BUSINESS MEETINGS THAT WORK

Copyright © 2018 by Dori Sella

Business Meetings That Work: 6 Steps to Increase Productivity

ISBN 978-965-90004-0-1 (print), 978-965-90004-1-8 (epub)

All rights reserved. This book or any portion thereof may not be reproduced or used in any manner whatsoever without the express written permission of the publisher except for the use of brief quotations in a book review.

1st Edition

Editor: Jami Bernard, Barncatpublishing.com

Publishing and Design Services: MartinPublishingServices.com

BUSINESS MEETINGS THAT WORK

6 STEPS TO INCREASE PRODUCTIVITY

DORI SELLA

to my family

Contents

INTRODUCTION 1
    What pilots can teach us about meetings 1
    A checklist for the rest of us 3
    All business meetings are sales meetings 5
    Some final notes about the 6-Step Checklist 8

THE 6-STEP CHECKLIST 11

6 STEPS TO BUSINESS MEETINGS THAT WORK 13

    STEP 1: OBJECTIVES 15
        Know where you are going 15
        Clarifying your objectives 17
        The 3 levels of objectives 19
        Other meeting attendees also have objectives 26
        Creating success criteria 32
        Plan B – Planning for the unexpected 38

STEP 2: PEOPLE 43

Who is participating? 43

The customer – Whom do you want to join the meeting? 44

Your company – Whom do you want to join the meeting? 52

The importance of internal alignment 56

Setting expectations 61

STEP 3: STATE OF MIND 65

Everything we do reflects our mindset 65

Attendees' SOM 67

Personal SOM 70

Gauging shifts in SOM 73

STEP 4: CONTENT 79

The what and how of achieving objectives 79

Time – What does it mean? 81

Content is more than just a presentation 84

Creating rapport: The HOW of getting your message across 92

Frames: Giving context to content 102

STEP 5: OBJECTIONS 107

An integral part of the sales process 107

Planning for objections 108

Preparing for NO objections 111

Bonus: Using language patterns to deal with objections 113

STEP 6: CLOSING 121
    It can be the most important part of a meeting 121
    Planning the closing 122
    Leaving an open door 126

GOING FORWARD 131

WILL USING THIS CHECKLIST HELP MY BOTTOM LINE? 137

EPILOGUE 139

ACKNOWLEDGEMENTS 141

REFERENCES 145

ABOUT THE AUTHOR 147

Worksheets

The worksheets are available for you to download from my site:

http://www.dorisella.com/book

Please scroll to the bottom of the page and enter the password:

6STEPS

I would love to hear your feedback.

Dori@dorisella.com

INTRODUCTION

What pilots can teach us about meetings

It was 6 a.m. and I was sitting in the cockpit of a Boeing 777 on my way to a meeting in Bucharest. I knew a lot of pilots from my days as an officer in the Air Force, and my pilot that day had invited me to join him in the cockpit for takeoff. I have been a cockpit guest on many planes, from a Fouga CM.170 Magister (a military combat trainer jet) to a Lockheed C-130 (a military transport plane), and dozens of small and large commercial aircraft — from two-seaters to Jumbo 747s. I am always mesmerized by the skill of the pilots as they navigate a huge piece of metal into the sky and bring it down again safely.

Inside the cockpit, there is a clear division of work. "APU?" calls out one pilot, reading from a pre-flight checklist.

"Off," the other one responds.

Flaps? Fifteen.

Flight controls? Checked.

Cabin crew? Signal.

Once the plane hits the runway, they switch to the takeoff checklist. There are words and phrases I recognize — "transponder," "clock," "above-400-foot radio" — and others that I don't. We lift into the sky, and the checklist continues until we reach cruising height.

I found myself wishing for the equivalent of a pilot's checklist once I arrived at my meeting in Bucharest. Although I had prepared for it — or thought I had — the meeting turned out to be a disaster. More people showed up than I had expected, each with a different agenda. The local agent had not prepared me well and I had not asked him the right questions. As a road warrior, always on the go and getting ready at the last minute, it's easy to forget some of the most basic questions to ask in advance.

I am by no means a newcomer to business meetings. Because I am an Excel freak, I have calculated that over a 33-year career, I have attended or led more than 7,500 customer sales meetings and another 22,000 internal meetings.

That's a lot of meetings! But I have a confession to make. Although I was physically present, in many of those meetings my mind had wandered off elsewhere. I might have been partly listening and partly checking my email. Many times, I could have been better prepared.

I'm not proud of this, but I am not alone. In one survey, 92 percent of employees admitted to spending time in meetings doing other work.

Everyone knows that most, well many, business meetings are a waste of time. The research bears this out. Salary.com reports that 47 percent of people surveyed say that ineffective meetings are the biggest drain on their time. A "Meetings of

America" report for Verizon Conferencing found that almost all attendees admitted to daydreaming during meetings, and over a third even admitted to dozing off. (I wonder how many dozed and *didn't* admit it.)

It is interesting to note that a survey of U.K. office workers by Opinion Matters for Epson found that it takes only about 11 minutes before attendees start to lose focus.

A study by Keyorganization.com found that one of the biggest contributors to stress in the workplace was attending too many meetings, and that up to 50 percent of meeting time is wasted.

There is a huge financial cost, too. One U.S. statistic estimates the annual salary cost for unnecessary meetings at $37 billion.

A checklist for the rest of us

The pilot's checklist was developed in the early 1940s when airplanes became more complex, and has been refined over the years. Most pilots can probably take off and land in their sleep — but no matter how experienced they are, they always review their checklists with utmost seriousness, and not just because it is required by law. Pilots report that they *like* using checklists. "It frees up my brain," one told me, so that he does not have to think about routine actions and instead can focus on core objectives.

Pilot checklists are not only about human error and safety. They also save time and ensure that the mission is completed. Those checklists were such a success that the concept has been introduced to many other fields.

For example, there are now checklists for patient intake at

hospitals, and checklists for before and during surgery, and even after surgery, so that all instruments are accounted for. A study of checklist implementation in surgery found a 30 percent relative reduction in major medical complications.

So, here's the question: Why isn't there a checklist for business meetings?

Although business meetings don't risk anyone's life, they do involve — just as in aviation and hospital procedures — linear steps that mostly take place before the "action" begins. Once the action starts, the process is complex and demands professionalism and skill. A well-prepared business executive — just like the pilot or the surgeon — will undoubtedly perform better when using a checklist, no matter the person's experience.

Other benefits of using a checklist for a business meeting include:

- saving time and money
- increasing mindfulness
- lowering stress/burnout
- improving efficiency, effectiveness, and the bottom line
- plus enhancing teamwork and handover, thereby minimizing avoidable errors and complications.

My idea to use a standard checklist for business meetings came to me when I started training sales people. I have watched organizations spend thousands of dollars (and more) to implement new methodologies, only to eventually drift back to the old bad habits. I wanted to bring to each of my trainings a consolidated checklist of the main points I believed were critical to the successful implementation of each topic.

Knowing that salespeople don't like to read a lot of material beforehand, or fill out complicated forms (even the pilot checklist cannot be too wordy or contain too many steps or it will become counter-productive), I came up with a simple, straightforward, user-friendly point of reference that would directly help companies and organizations achieve their goals.

The result is the **6-Step Checklist**. It will not burden your day or add to your workload. Instead, using the **6-Step Checklist** will make your life easier and bring tangible results. It will help you take quick and obvious — yet critical — steps that make the most of every stakeholder's valuable time. At the same time, when you have a complex meeting you will find important details to help you move beyond the obvious.

"...SIMPLE, STRAIGHTFORWARD, USER-FRIENDLY POINT OF REFERENCE THAT WOULD DIRECTLY HELP COMPANIES AND ORGANIZATIONS ACHIEVE THEIR GOALS."

All business meetings are sales meetings

The **6-Step Checklist** is simple and flexible enough to use at virtually any meeting, even those that are not strictly "sales" meetings.

Actually, every business meeting is in some way a sales meeting. Even if you are not technically in "sales," you are conducting or participating in sales meetings all day long. Asking and getting approval or agreement on priorities involves selling your idea/project. Job interviews and dates are sales meetings; **what you are selling is you**. You are selling yourself when you ask for a raise or a promotion. You are selling your experience, your contribution, and your potential contribution. You are selling your abilities and your skills.

A sales meeting is a meeting in which one side wants to influence the other to make a change toward an ultimate business goal. These meetings include all traditional transaction-based sales meetings, not unlike an artist meeting with an agent, or a doctor in a hospital discussing budgets/resources and approvals, or a volunteer in an NGO needing budget approval. All of these are business meetings that are actually sales meetings.

Within these meetings, much can happen: gathering information, introducing a new concept/product/solution, negotiating resources (money/time/people etc.), getting approvals (budget, concept development, job offer), signing a contract.

At a recent workshop with medical device sales people, we were discussing how most business meetings are sales meetings. One of the sales reps raised his hand and said, "I have many meetings that aren't 'sales meetings' with the doctors. Only once a quarter do I have a sales meeting. All the other meetings I have with the doctors are to build the relationship, but I'm not 'selling.'"

I realized immediately that we needed to **reframe the word "sales."** To many people, a "sales meeting" involves the actual negotiating and signing of a contract, and/or the actual transfer of funds. Let's widen that to include any type of meeting with a potential customer. **It is a sales meeting when you want something to change that will move you closer to your ultimate goal.** This can be as basic as wanting to strengthen a relationship and create a more personal bond. Or getting information, changing a perception, educating, raising awareness, impressing, getting a grant or approval, passing an exam, introducing a new concept, securing a raise — and of course, getting an agreement to purchase something.

If you are socially friendly with your customer, you probably don't want to have a "sales meeting" while you're out at a show and dinner with your spouses and other friends (though this often happens anyway). However, when you invite your client to play golf or watch a football game, you are most definitely in a "sales meeting." There are clear roles of who is the host and who is the customer. Your behavior, as relaxed as it may be, will still be different than if you were just out with friends.

Now that we have established that every meeting with a customer in the sales process is a sales meeting, what about the internal business meetings that occur within companies? Are they also sales meetings?

For the purpose of this book, I am differentiating between a "business meeting" and a "professional meeting." A professional meeting's goal is to learn, brainstorm, and discuss. It involves sharing information and knowledge regarding the specific professional area (e.g., patient health versus budget approval, technical specifications versus prioritization of work). Even for a professional meeting, you will find that the **6-Step Checklist** is helpful. However, this book will focus on business meetings.

An internal meeting where you want to convince people to give priority to your topic or get approval and agreement on your idea of how to do something — that is a sales meeting. The same is true for a job interview or when asking for a raise, which is about selling yourself.

"Selling" is sometimes considered negative. But when it's understood in the context of making a change to move closer to achieving a mutual goal, then perhaps it can help you feel more comfortable about the process.

A 2017 article by Jeff Haden in *Inc.* magazine takes it a step further: *"Any meeting that won't directly generate revenue or cost savings — either in the form of a key decision or a concrete plan of action — is a complete waste of money."*

Some final notes about the 6-Step Checklist

The **6-Step Checklist** is quick, practical, and easy to use. It is relevant to all types of business/sales meetings, each of which we will address in our checklist methodology chapters: Complex B2B sales meetings, internal business meetings, and job interviews.

In addition to a detailed explanation of each of the checklist elements, each chapter offers examples (Practical Use), tips and guidelines, as well as a worksheet to help you personalize the checklist for your specific meeting.

Before plunging in, you might be wondering whether using such a checklist is worth the effort. I have trained dozens and dozens of people to use this **6-Step Checklist**, and they have **all** reported back to me that it helped them enormously in terms of **focus, state of mind, preparation, and results**.

They report feeling better about themselves as they head into their meetings, knowing what they want to get out of them and how they are going to achieve it. They like that the checklist is holistic and modular, that it does not have to be used dogmatically but can be applied with common sense, and that it covers core business issues while also dealing with the personal, human aspect of making a meeting successful.

One of the biggest surprises for me has been hearing from friends in the arts. They, too, benefit from the checklist. Even if their main profession is not "sales," per se, artists and independents have to meet with their agents, who help them with their business. Artists concern themselves with the creative aspects of their work, but they still have to *sell* their work, or sell agents on selling their work for them.

Selling is something we do naturally in every meeting, but especially in business meetings. Being prepared for every meeting, even if it's only focusing on the objective and the state of mind, will save on financial resources, increase mindfulness, lower stress and burnout — while also increasing the bottom line.

So, let's get started.

Do I have to use the entire checklist every time?

You can choose when you want or need to do the full checklist versus a bare-minimum checklist based on the type of meeting you are having. After a review of the full methodology and the different sub-checklists found in the Worksheets, there is a guideline of when to use which one and specific points to consider when on the phone/web or a chance meeting in the hallway or at an event.

DEFINITIONS

The following are definitions of some of the terms we will be using often in this book as we examine how to apply the 6-Step Checklist to different sales scenarios:

Complex Business-to-Business Sales Process Meeting (Complex B2B)

One of the main attributes of a Complex B2B sales process is that the decision process involves multiple departments within the customer's organization, and the sale is made to many different people (with different agendas). Meetings are usually face-to-face, but can be on video/conference call as well.

Internal Meeting

A meeting held within an organization, where all participants are employed by the same organization, and which may include people in different countries. This meeting also can be face to face or via video/conference call.

Job Interview (also, request for a raise)

This includes any situation where you want to make a change in your work environment, such as getting hired by a new company, asking for a raise, making a change within your company, and asking for more benefits or recognition.

Account Team

In a Complex B2B sales process there will usually be a customer "account team" that consists of a sales person, perhaps a technical/clinical expert, a project manager, and multiple other people within the organization who may be brought into the sales process to move that process forward, depending on the size and complexity of the opportunity.

THE 6-STEP CHECKLIST

1. **OBJECTIVES**
   - ☐ Define medium-range and specific, immediate meeting objectives
   - ☐ Consider attendee objectives
   - ☐ Define success criteria
   - ☐ Create Plan B: planning for the unexpected

2. **PEOPLE**
   - ☐ Define and verify who attends (customer/external)
   - ☐ Define and verify who is joining me (internal), and who will help me
   - ☐ Verify internal alignment is complete
   - ☐ Verify expectations with all attendees

3. **STATE OF MIND (SOM)**
   - ☐ Define expected and desired SOM (attendees)
   - ☐ Define and evaluate my desired personal SOM to maintain control of meeting
   - ☐ Review SOM with other attendees
   - ☐ Review ways to gauge movement from SOM to SOM

4. **CONTENT**
   - ☐ Review time constraints
   - ☐ Define main points to be covered
   - ☐ Define your questions
   - ☐ Define ways to create and maintain rapport
   - ☐ Develop Story Frames

5. **OBJECTIONS**
   - ☐ Define potential objections and craft answers
   - ☐ Create questions/stories to help hear objections
   - ☐ Review language patterns to prepare for objections

6. **CLOSING**
   - ☐ Plan the closing
   - ☐ Define desired Action Items
   - ☐ Define "Leave an Open Door" strategy

6 STEPS TO BUSINESS MEETINGS THAT WORK

STEP 1: OBJECTIVES

Know where you are going

If you get nothing else from this book, at least come away with this: **All meetings begin with an objective**. If you don't know where you are going, how will you get there? What is it that you want to get out of this meeting?

That said, it's not always so easy to define your objective. There are different types of objectives in general and different objectives for every person you will meet. Objectives are meaningless if they do not have any measurable success criteria. Also, you will need a Plan B in case your original objectives can not be met.

DEFINITIONS

Long-Range objective
This can be considered the overall vision — not necessarily achievable, but always in mind.

Medium-Range objective
Something tangible, specific, with a timeframe (e.g. a sales pipeline entry, a project with a deadline, getting hired).

Specific meeting objective
This is what you want to happen as a direct outcome of a specific meeting. This objective will move you closer to your medium-range objective.

Stated objective
One that is clearly expressed and available to all. Often, it is re-stated at the beginning of a meeting to set the stage for discussion.

Hidden objective
An unstated objective that is known by only one or a limited number of people. Usually, but not always, secondary to the Stated Objective; sometimes the Stated Objective is just a cover for the Hidden Objective.

Plan B
Planning for the unexpected. What is the minimum you hope to achieve at this meeting if you fall short of your Specific Objective?

Clarifying your objectives

Many years ago, on a cold and rainy night near Dusseldorf, nine people I worked with from a service vendor, were preparing for a business meeting with a large German company the following day, at a hotel on the outskirts of the city.

Each person from my company had a different objective. Three of them came from product organizations, wanting to sell their product or at least get feedback only on their product. Two were concerned with how they would deliver the products that had already been sold. I had been brought in to present the results of research we had conducted, with the objective of creating a need for new service. The rest of the team was probably just along for the ride, and the senior German executive from my company was looking at the long-term relationship and value of such an important customer.

In our internal four-hour preparation, with team members joining as they flew in from different countries, we talked a lot about what we were going to do and how we would present it. We spent hours of energy on making sure the presentations looked nice.

But, we never stopped to talk about WHY we were there. What was our objective as a team? Nor did we designate a leader for the upcoming meeting. We made sure that all the fonts matched, but we didn't stop to clarify why we were meeting in the first place, or to align our objectives and stories.

The following day all nine of us got to the meeting, where another 12 people joined us. All through the six-hour meeting at the German company's offices members of both companies walked in and out, while some got separate work done on their computers while sitting at the meeting.

Needless to say, it was a huge waste of time, money, personnel and resources for both companies. Nothing of substance came out of this meeting.

I have sat in on literally hundreds of internal preparations for customer meetings where everyone takes for granted that the objective of the specific meeting is clear, as are the medium-range and the long-term objectives.

This is rarely the case.

When objectives are discussed, most people focus on the WHAT and HOW, and less on the WHY. At best, they look ahead to the medium-range goal ("make a sale") or the tactical ("establish a relationship"), but there are many stages in between that are usually (perhaps always) overlooked. True, some of these missing objectives are harder to define and may demand an extra moment of consideration and focus; nevertheless, they are critical to tackle.

Most sales people would say that their long-term goal is to become the vendor of choice, bringing value to the customer and having repeat sales. The mid-range objective is also relatively simple — to sell x product for y $ by T time. They are not as clear on the desired outcome of any specific meeting. They find it easier to focus on WHAT they are going to do, and remain vague, even to themselves, on WHY they are doing it.

Defining the desired outcome of a meeting, using specific and measurable objectives, will help you move forward in the sales process and enable you to make adjustments as needed along the way.

> **Objectives and agendas are not the same thing!**
>
> The Agenda is WHAT you agree you are going to talk about, including when and how much time you will allocate per topic. Objectives are WHY you are talking about this in the first place, and what you want to get out of the discussion.
>
> See more about Agendas in the chapter on Content.

The 3 levels of objectives

In a Complex B2B sales situation, where multiple people and departments are involved, there are most likely three levels of objectives:

Long-Range objective

The long-term vision is always relevant and perhaps never 100 percent attainable. But it is the ultimate goal of all your meetings and can be something that is generic yet vital, and important to remember. Example: "To have a satisfied customer who will see us as trusted advisors and look to us to continue to supply them with solutions to advance their business in the future."

When the Long-Term Objective is the guiding objective for all meetings, it allows for the flexibility to make changes as needed and still stay focused on where you are going. Sometimes it's worthwhile to remind all of your company's participants about this goal.

Medium-Range objective

In a Complex B2B sales meeting, this would be the sale you want to make. It probably consists of a product, solution, monetary figure and specific time frame, and should also have a value to the customer. "Sell solution Z for $XXX by Q3XX to company Y that will benefit company Y by such-and-such time."

Specific meeting objective

If it is a "closing meeting," then the objective is obviously "to get a commitment on the product, solution or idea I want to sell."

However, in most Complex B2B sales meetings with multiple participants, you will have many meetings. Some will be face to face, some will be formal and some informal, some on the phone, some on the Web or even via email. Each time you have contact with your customer you should be focused on what it is you want to achieve with this interaction. If you want to be pals, do that on your own time! But if the reason you are meeting is to create a transaction between two companies, then your specific objective should always be to move forward toward your medium-range or long-range objective.

PRACTICAL USE

The 3 levels of objectives

 Complex B2B sales meeting

Long-Range objective

"Customer will see us as a trusted advisor and look to us for continuing to supply them with solutions that will advance their business."

Medium-Range objective

"Sell $XXX of a specific product or solution by end of quarter."

Specific meeting objective

To formulate this objective, ask yourself this question: What will advance me in the sales cycle?

Some possibilities:

- "Create a need" (by sharing market trends or case studies)
- "Get information about the buying process" (this could even happen over a meal)
- "Change perception of type of solution for specific problems" (introduce alternative solution)
- "Get agreement on financial/legal terms of sale"

PRACTICAL USE

The 3 levels of objectives, cont.

 **Internal meeting**

Long-Range objective

This would be related to the specific values of the company and the way the company does business, and would probably always include something related to *working together to create value for customers*. This is important to remember, as the ultimate goal of any business is to create value for its customers so they have reason for making a transaction. *It can only happen if people work together.* Going into an internal meeting with this objective in mind can help keep perspective when personal agendas that create tension get caught up in the professional world.

Medium-Range objective

Complete a specific task/mission in the most efficient and effective manner.

Specific meeting objective

What will help me advance toward my goal? (versus making someone feel bad, blaming others for not doing their job, or fighting over priorities)

Some possibilities:

- "Set priorities"
- "Get commitment to develop/continue project"
- "Explore new ideas"
- "Review Action Items"

PRACTICAL USE

The 3 levels of objectives, cont.

 Job Interview/Request a raise

Long-Range objective

This would ideally be related to finding a job that is both satisfying and rewarding, which will mean something specific to each person individually.

Medium-Range objective

Get a job offer within timeline.

Specific interview objective

What needs to happen to move me closer to getting the job offer?

- Impress interviewer that you are the best candidate
- Find out more about the job demands, people, company culture, etc.
- Land a second interview

Defining specific meeting objectives

SINCE DEFINING THE SPECIFIC MEETING OBJECTIVE is the most important thing you can do — and often the hardest — here are some ideas.

The question becomes: What is the objective for this specific meeting that will move you forward in the sales process?

When preparing for a meeting, you probably don't have to reiterate your Medium-Range Objective, although when multiple people are participating it is usually a good idea to make sure everyone is on the same page. However, when it comes to the Specific Objective for a particular meeting, everyone should be in sync.

Ask yourself what needs to happen here that will move you toward your Medium-Range Objective (moving forward in the sales process). What do you want to achieve in this meeting? Gather information? Create interest? Change perception? How will you know if you achieved it?

Literally imagine the end of the meeting — how people look, what they are saying, how they feel. Also envision how YOU will look, what you will say, how you will feel. This helps clarify the objective for the specific meeting.

"Good relationships" are not enough

At one time, just spending time with a customer and establishing a relationship might have been enough. Today, with the overload of information that we thought would make our lives less cluttered, it is more important than ever to make sure we are clear on why we are taking our valuable time and that of our customers to engage. Meeting just to chat is disrespectful of your customer's time (and your employers). That doesn't mean that you don't need to have a good relationship with your customer; it means that the good relationship should be based on bringing value to your customer that is related to both your businesses.

Delivering a presentation is never the objective!

Delivering a presentation is NEVER an objective – it's a means. When focusing on the WHAT, often the objective becomes "making the presentation." I went with two very experienced former C-level businessmen who had founded a start-up and were going to a meeting with a potential investor. I asked them what their objective was and one of them answered, "What do you mean? Of course it's to deliver the presentation of our company. That's why we're here."

"Okay," I said. "But what happens if the investor walks into the room and announces that he's read all about your work and he's ready to invest right that second. Do you still make that presentation?"

We are all blind when we are involved in something that is important to us personally, such as when we have to sell an idea that we came up with, or sell ourselves in an interview. We get over-involved with the content and forget the objective. I am no exception. Another reason why we need the **6-Step Checklist**.

Other meeting attendees also have objectives

While it's vital to know what we want to get out of meetings, we can become so preoccupied with our own goals that we forget there are other people in the room, and that what they want may be different from what we want.

The most amazing situation I ever witnessed was when the founders of a start-up company, both of them experienced executives, asked me to join them in meeting a representative from the Mobile World Congress (MWC) who was visiting in their country. They wanted my opinion of the meeting. Their goal was to get the visitor to give them a spot in the new innovation section of the exhibition.

They sat down at the meeting and immediately began to bombard the MWC representative with how wonderful and innovative their newly invented technology was and what a great addition it would be to the MWC. During a ten-minute monologue by the start-up's CEO, I realized that the MWC representative was listening politely, but was not at all engaged. I asked him about his role at the MWC and it turned out that he was a salesperson looking for sponsorships.

Most situations don't involve such a blatant mismatch, but I have often been in meetings where the parties were not on the same page at all. It shows how important it is to do the homework — and that includes finding out what's in it for the other attendees, or at least making an educated guess.

What are *their* objectives? Knowing this will give you, as the leader of the meeting, an advantage in your planning in terms of being better prepared, more on point, and able to listen with more "tools" to hear your customer's real objective.

It also helps you see more clearly by taking you out of your own head and into a different perspective or point of view. Having more than one point of view is a key to being flexible. And being flexible is a key attribute of a successful meeting leader — especially in a sales situation. Having several options gives us the flexibility to check and validate the customer's objective and ensure that you have the control to help align goals and expectations.

The best way to get initial information is to discuss the agenda with your main contact and ask what the participants' expectations are. What do they want to get out of the meeting? If they tell you straight out — great! But note that even when they tell you their objectives, there is very likely a hidden objective they are not as willing to share.

Information on your attendees' objectives is not always available. That is one of the reasons we use champions within an organization to give us information. Even with the aid of a champion, sometimes this is where guesswork comes in: It is up to you to make an educated guess. It may not sound scientific, but it's important.

When you do your guesswork, it opens you and your team up to listening for key words and reactions that help you discover these hidden objectives. Make your best guess in advance, and clarify during the meeting.

Reading the latest news on the company can help you find information. It's always a good idea to check LinkedIn and other social media to learn as much as you can about other attendees.

"YOU WILL HAVE AN ADVANTAGE IF YOU GUESS AT AND ARE REALISTIC ABOUT HIDDEN OBJECTIVES."

Even when you have good inside information, don't expect to meet all of the objectives. You will have an advantage if you guess at and are realistic about hidden objectives. This is where internal brainstorming as well as role-playing with your team and other experienced people within your company can help. They can give different perspectives and help you better prepare for your attendees' stated and hidden objectives.

PRACTICAL USE

Making an educated guess

 Complex B2B sales meeting

Depending on the stage of the sales process, how well you know your customer, and what type of information you have from internal customer resources, you can probably make some educated guesses about both the stated and the hidden objectives.

Their stated objectives:

- Learn about new trends in the market
- Get a solution for a specific problem
- Evaluate how you can deliver a solution compared to your competitors
- Sell you something (don't laugh - I have been to more than one meeting where the person attending from the "customer" side actually wanted to sell a service.)

Their hidden objectives:

- Learn about new technologies/trends so they can develop internally
- Put pressure on you to lower your price
- Get information to give to competitor regarding features/price/timeline

When you prepare and even make a guess at what could be the hidden objectives, you and your team will become better listeners during the meeting for nuances that can give you important advantages.

PRACTICAL USE

Making an educated guess, Cont.

 Internal meeting

Even though you are all in the same company, each of the other attendees will probably have different objectives — especially the hidden ones. The stated objective may be the agenda, but understanding the hidden objectives will help meeting leaders achieve their own objectives more efficiently. It also enables leaders to address potential issues in general, and at least set the frame for the core objective by using a lot of rapport (see more on this in the Content chapter).

Examples of hidden objectives:

- Get recognition for idea/job done — people often complain about those who join meetings solely to "steal ideas" or at least promote themselves with the organization
- Job security — can cause people to push certain agendas and reduce cooperation
- Different priorities and pressures — can create a situation where people are not able to move forward toward objective of meeting

"HAVING AN OBJECTIVE THAT IS CUSTOMER-FOCUSED ALREADY CREATES VALUE AND CAN HELP YOU DIFFERENTIATE YOURSELF FROM COMPETITORS."

PRACTICAL USE

Making an educated guess, cont.

 Job interview/Request a raise

When you go on an interview, it's important to know who is interviewing you, as that person will have very different objectives depending on their role in the organization. A human-resources interviewer will be looking for a candidate who has the skills and can fit in with the company culture and work well with specific teams, as well as have a place to grow and incentive to work for at least as long as it takes to make a significant contribution (depending on the position).

A professional manager wants to find the right candidate who has the maximum knowledge/skills/experience to do the job well, and usually also considers how quickly the applicant can ramp up and be ready to contribute. Hidden objectives for a manager could include a personal preference for another candidate or a desire to wrap up as quickly as possible, especially if the decision has been made in advance.

I once interviewed for a position where it was clear that the interviewer had already made a decision on a candidate. I continued anyway, as I knew he didn't have the final say, but I also knew that I would have to work with him and it would be much better if he saw the value I could bring to the position versus the other candidate. I had prepared many questions about problems he could possibly be having that would be my responsibility to address. Very quickly we left the realm of the traditional interview and got into a "real conversation" about problems and solutions. He offered me the job.

> **Meeting a new customer**
>
> When meeting a new customer, the traditional objective most salespeople would cite is: "Get to know the customers and their needs." But, assuming your underlying objective is to make sure the customer sees/understands the value you bring, the objective is really: "**Show customers you can bring them value.**" (How you can do that will be discussed in the chapter on Content.)
>
> Having an objective that is customer-focused already creates value and can help you differentiate yourself from competitors. To do this, you need to get to know the customer … but there is plenty you can find out beforehand by using LinkedIn and Google.
>
> Also helpful: Check to see what conferences the company speaks at regarding your topic, or what topics have been discussed locally in regard to your area of expertise. You can pleasantly surprise the customer with new and valuable information that helps them do their job better.

Creating success criteria

Having an objective is like defining where you are going on a map, including your specific objectives for each segment of the trip.

While driving south from New York to Orlando, you might have a daily objective to stop for a break in Delaware and rest for the night in Richmond. Here, your success criteria would be to arrive in Delaware for lunch and to arrive in Richmond after dinner.

In a sales meeting, it isn't always so clear how to measure success, especially if the goal is to change perception from negative to positive. If they smile nicely and say thank you, did you succeed in changing their perception? You don't really know. Maybe they are just being polite.

Defining in advance the "cues" you need to see or hear, and planning to watch or listen to them, will help ensure that you have reached your goal.

Let's say you want to change perception regarding the ability of your solution to help the customer resolve a problem. If you start hearing questions that include the words "if we use your solution will we be able to…," you know that there is some consideration and that you have created an initial change.

Body language is also an indicator of change. Another indicator is an introduction to someone within the organization whom you have not previously met, especially if it's someone you have targeted.

How do you know it was a good meeting?

Let's imagine a meeting where you deliver a presentation, everyone claps and says thank you, and then everyone indulges in pleasant small talk. A few questions are asked and you answer them all. You don't hear any major objections, and there is a smile on every face. The good-byes are cordial. Was it a good meeting?

In all fairness, there isn't enough information to go on here — and that is the point. How did you define "success" while planning and preparing for the meeting? It is totally legitimate to evaluate at the end of the meeting what you got from it and what you want to do with any new information, but that does not supplant having a clear list of success criteria to help you measure and evaluate your success.

DEFINITION

The decision-making process

The decision-making process refers to who needs to approve and what structures are in place in order to move from one step to the next. The decision criteria are the motivations for the decision like the timeliness of delivery, a certain feature, roadmap, ease of installation. The process and the criteria are separate from the "compelling event" — why the customer needs the solution/product in the first place and what is at stake.

Setting success criteria

THE QUESTION YOU ARE ASKING is, "How will I know that I have achieved my objective for this meeting? What needs to happen that will enable me to say that I have achieved what I wanted to achieve?"

Needless to say, any interpretation of "success" must be connected to your initial objectives.

Let's take a look at some examples of success criteria:

 Complex B2B sales meeting

OBJECTIVE	SUCCESS CRITERIA
Create a need (by sharing market trends or case studies)	Agreement to run a POC (Proof of Concept) Get an introduction to someone else in the organization
Get information about the buying process (this may happen over a meal)	Gain specific information (decision-making process and/or decision criteria)
Change perception of type of solution for specific problems (introduce alternative solutions)	Successfully answered objections Clear "identification" with the solution: "So if we use this like this it can help us do xx? And will answer our problem Y?" Asking a direct question as to what they think and how they would implement your idea/solution
Agree on financial/legal terms of sale	Signed or verbal agreement on all apsects

Setting success criteria, cont.

Internal meeting

OBJECTIVE	SUCCESS CRITERIA
Set priorities	Priorities agreed upon and defined, with follow-up action items
Review Action Items	Previous action items resolved New action items clear, documented and dated with an owner
Get commitment to develop/continue project	Approval received Project status reviewed; problems identified/resolved
Explore new ideas	New ideas documented with action items

Setting success criteria, cont.

 Job interview/Request a raise

Obviously you would like to get a job offer or at least some feedback, and you have no direct control over this, but there are some success criteria you can pre-define based on your objectives:

OBJECTIVE	ACTION
Impress interviewer that you are the best candidate	Positive feedback from interviewer Discussion of next steps
Find out more about the job demands, people, company, culture, etc.	Getting answers to questions, keeping in mind that an experienced interviewer will give you very little information
Get a second interview	Having a date for the next interview, along with name of individual

Plan B – Planning for the unexpected

At a meeting in London with a satellite company, I walked into a room with 25 people, where I was supposed to talk to them about the business rationale behind using voicemail. At the time, I was inexperienced and we didn't clearly discuss objectives, nor did I ask the best questions beforehand about the customer.

Once I began talking with them, I asked how their network worked. I soon understood that, with the way they provided service, they had no need whatsoever for voicemail. It would be a total waste of their time if I started explaining the business rationale and how to use it.

What did I do? I reminded myself of the long-range objective — that they continue to buy from our company and see us as trusted advisors. I asked them questions in areas of my expertise where I knew I could add value, and opened a discussion. AND I learned a huge lesson on preparation and expectations.

Meetings are with people, and people are complex. It's impossible to have control over everything that happens. However, the more prepared you are, the more flexible you will be so that you can make the most of every meeting.

Previously, we talked about three layers of objectives: the long-range objective (or vision), the medium-range objective (usually the target goal), and the specific objective of the meeting (usually a means to getting to the target). Keeping the long-range vision in mind is what enables top sales people — and top performers in general — to excel at meetings and always get something of value out of any scenario.

It is always worthwhile to plan in advance what might go

wrong and how you may want to react in such a situation. I have found that when you realize that you will not be able to achieve your initial objective, the best course of action is to keep your larger goal in mind, and to ask questions and listen for ways you can best bring value. What you don't want to do is just finish your presentation and run for the door. Having such a Plan B at the ready will maximize your chances of having an effective meeting, no matter how unexpectedly bumpy the road.

PRACTICAL USE

When things don't go right, cont.

 Complex B2B sales meeting

Most experienced sales people prepare for different scenarios (Plan B) before a negotiation or when going to a meeting where they know the customer has a complaint. On a business trip to New Zealand with a C-level executive, we arrived at the meeting to find that his counterpart did not show up. During our advance preparation, we decided that if the executive had additional time, (Plan B) he would join the other meetings to learn more about what was happening in the field (which was the larger goal of the trip. When his counterpart didn't show up, he immediately joined the technical meeting and made sure to make the most of the long journey.

You may find yourself in a situation where the customer will stop your presentation and say they are not interested in your product/solution, despite the fact that they approved the meeting and you traveled far to make it. A deep breath and making the best of it is often all you can do.

 Internal meeting

When another crisis in the organization has completely changed the company's priorities, and some of the people attending have shifted their priorities as well, it is imperative to acknowledge the crisis and ask if it's possible for a short time to continue on your topic. If not, reschedule.

PRACTICAL USE

When things don't go right, cont.

 Job interview/Request a Raise

What if you arrive at a one-on-one interview, only to find it has turned into a group interview? Your choice is whether to go with the flow or refuse to participate or if you find the interviewer is pre-occupied, find an appropriate time and ask whether it would be okay to come back another time.

STOP! Is this meeting necessary?

The more you meet your customers face-to-face in sales, the better — although there are rare occasions when meeting can actually sabotage a process, as during negotiations when waiting is a tactical decision. However, when it comes to internal meetings, I have no doubt that anyone who has been in an organization knows how much time is wasted on unnecessary meetings.

RULE OF THUMB: When there is a problem, always do your best to meet in person (or pick up the phone), both with customers and your colleagues.

Download the worksheet pack at http://www.dorisella.com/book
Password: 6STEPS

BUSINESS MEETINGS THAT WORK

Worksheet 1: Objectives

Name of Customer _____ Date of Meeting _____

Objectives Checklist

- ☐ Define medium-range and specific, immediate meeting objectives
- ☐ Consider attendee objectives
- ☐ Define success criteria
- ☐ Create Plan B: planning for the unexpected

Mid-Range Objective

What is my mid-range objective (in sales – usually what's in the pipeline)

_____

Specific Meeting Objectives

What do I want to happen at the end of this specific meeting?

1. _____
2. _____
3. _____
4. _____

Attendees Objectives

Stated Objectives _____

_____

Hidden Objectives _____

_____

Success Criteria - How will I determine at the end of the meeting that it was successful?

1. _____
2. _____
3. _____

Plan B – Flexibility – Overlay goal and minimum outcome

1. _____
2. _____

Copyright 2018 © | info@dorisella.com

STEP 2: PEOPLE

Who is participating?

It seems so obvious. Still, to make the meeting effective, you need to do your best to get the right people in the room and at least know who else is going to be attending your meeting.

What makes a meeting a meeting is that it takes place between *people*, not just between businesses. This chapter focuses on the importance of choosing and defining which people should attend the meeting to help you achieve your goals.

What is their role in the meeting? What is their role in advancing you to your objective? This includes attention to who should join you from the customer side and who should join you from your own company.

This chapter will also review the importance of internal alignment (within your company) and setting expectations with your customer in advance so as to achieve maximum efficiency.

DEFINITIONS

Customer attendees

In this context, it is the person — a customer, a job interviewer, or people within your organization — to whom you need to sell a concept or get an approval.

Internal attendees

Your supporters are all those who are there to help you achieve your objectives. In a vendor-customer situation, that's everyone in your organization. At an in-company internal meeting, it would be people from your department who are helping you achieve a goal.

Relationship

In a Complex B2B situation the relationship is traditionally defined by how well you know the person, that person's position in the decision making process for this specific objective, and their affinity to your company's solution.

The customer – Whom do you want to join the meeting?

Many business meetings are held with the "wrong" people, those who have nothing to do with the issue at hand, or who are otherwise unable to move the topic forward toward an actual transaction or conclusion. For any type of meeting — whether a sales meeting, job interview, or even an internal meeting it is critical to know whom you want to or need to meet, who else is planning on being there, and what everyone's role is in their organization and in influencing the decision. This knowledge can make or break your success.

In the ideal situation, once you have defined your objective, it's easier to define which "titles" within the customer organization you want to meet. Is it someone from finance/purchasing? Someone technical or from marketing? Do you need someone senior or someone who understands the bits and bytes?

For example, in a Complex B2B meeting, if more than one department will use the solution you are selling, you will probably want to have people from all the relevant departments, perhaps department heads as well. If you have found out that there are people from finance who need to understand the solution, you may want non-technical people along to explain the business sense behind your solution. Depending on the seniority of the people you want to join, you may need to bring a counterpart from your company.

We don't live in an ideal world and you won't always know in advance who will be attending. Nevertheless, pre-qualifying and just asking questions can save a lot of time. Maybe there is a lot of discussion on whether you need to continue meeting with the "owner" of your solution, who is somehow blocking you from moving forward. They might be telling you that they don't have the budget, or that there is another supplier and your solution is not needed.

I often hear salespeople say they don't want to ruin the relationship by going past someone who is blocking them. I get it, but at the end of the day you are there to move forward on your objectives. If your sole objective is keeping the blocker happy, then by all means stay there … but if it's to find the right people to help you move toward a specific objective, you will need to find another way to get the right people and make it worth their while to meet with you.

When you know who is attending, you have an opportunity to review and discuss your relationship to those individuals.

> ### Sending a PowerPoint Presentation in advance
>
> One of the questions I get asked a lot is whether to send the PowerPoint presentation in advance. My answer is two-fold.
>
> First, does sending it in advance help your objectives or hinder them? If a preview of the presentation causes people to get locked into a particular mindset, then you probably don't want to send anything in advance.
>
> Second, are you required — either by protocol or customer request — to send something in advance? If so, send only the minimum that is required. If everything needs to be sent in advance, you will have to use attention-getting tactics, during the meeting to ensure that your points are correctly understood.

Defining customer participants

 Complex B2B sales meetings

Know your relationships

In a Complex B2B sales process, your relationship status to the people you're meeting traditionally consists of how well you know them, how relevant they are to your specific goal, what their role is in the decision-making process and also the all-important "friendliness" measure that is rated on a scale of 1 to 5. The highest score, 5, is for the Champion, the person who is willing to go above and beyond to make sure you can close your transaction. The lowest score, 1, is for the Enemy, who is most likely your competitor's champion.

In the middle of this scale is 3, a Neutral person, neither for you nor against you. Numbers 2 and 4 veer toward their respective ends of the scale.

This relationship scaling is also relevant when you are trying to get an approval within your company, interviewing for a job, or even when you are talking to your agent. How much are they invested in helping you move ahead? Who or what else are they promoting that could interfere with what you want?

"THIS RELATIONSHIP SCALING IS ALSO RELEVANT WHEN YOU ARE TRYING TO GET AN APPROVAL WITHIN YOUR COMPANY, INTERVIEWING FOR A JOB, OR EVEN WHEN YOU ARE TALKING TO YOUR AGENT."

Defining customer participants, cont.

In a Complex B2B sales process, the sale is to more than one person. You therefore need to have relationships with more than one person, including with those who can help you "sell" your solution within the organization. *The Challenger*, by Matthew Dixon and Brent Adamson, emphasizes that top performers target the people who are "change drivers" within their organization — people who are not usually the classic Champion, but rather the *Go-Getter* and the *Skeptic* who can actually drive the organization to making a decision.

Work with more than one person

When choosing in this situation who needs to be in your meeting to help you move forward, look beyond the classic Champion to other people within the organization. Bear in mind that company dynamics and responsibilities can change quickly and unexpectedly. Therefore, having relationships with multiple people in an organization is good practice.

Too senior can be detrimental

Sometimes having a contact who is *too* senior is not helpful in moving you forward in a sales process. That executive may be the final decision maker, but not the technical expert who is ultimately responsible for the use of the product/solution, and whose recommendation in the process is vital. You are much more likely to hear open feedback and information when you meet with your counterparts in an organization versus having the executives in the room.

A company I was working with was looking to expand into

Defining customer participants, cont.

the Italian market and had a meeting with a C-level executive of a major Italian manufacturer. During the meeting, the C-level executive showed a lot of interest in the solution the company was developing; asking questions and even providing a name of someone to talk to within his organization. The company executives I was working with were ecstatic that a senior executive from Italy had given his approval.

The reality is that this meeting, though pleasant, was useless. It may have been nice meeting with a C-level executive, but in this case he was too senior and strategic to be able to help a small company sell to a huge organization.

After a bit of detective work (and a lot of experience working with large organizations), we found out that the executive had sent the company I worked with on a wild goose chase to a department that was interested in developing in-house products and was mostly interested in picking brains. We had to start from scratch and find the department that would most benefit from the solution, and restart the process from the beginning. Had they not been so dazzled by the executive meeting, they would have figured this out much earlier and set different objectives for the meeting with the C-level executive.

Deal with blockers/gatekeepers

Anyone who has been in a sales process knows what it is like to run into a Blocker who just won't let you advance in the sales process. It could be an administrative assistant who won't let you talk to the executive, or a decision maker who won't consider your solution and won't let you meet with others who might.

Defining customer participants, cont.

In these situations, stay focused on your objective. Intelligently, with much consideration, find the way to get past these Blockers. For example, bring new value, bring executives or other professionals to meet with other people in the organization, or meet with other people at conferences and exhibitions.

Also, the more you know about all the influential people who can affect your sale, the more control you have over the process.

 Internal Meeting

The customer in this case would be the person or group you want to sell your idea to, in order to receive resources, approval, priority, etc. It could be someone more senior or from a different department. It could even be your own direct manager.

Treating your internal colleagues as customers — with the same eye toward bringing them value, for example — can help you be more efficient and effective. You may need to bring your direct line managers to a meeting in order to influence another senior manager. You will still be the leader of the meeting, even if it seems as if your senior managers are leading it and therefore hold the responsibility for making sure you are preparing everyone and making adjustments as best you can.

Defining customer participants, cont.

 Job interview/Request a raise

You don't usually have control over whom you are meeting; however, you should do as much research as you can to find out the title of the person and what their focus would be in the interview. LinkedIn is a great place to start, as well as simply Googling the company and gathering whatever information you can.

"TREATING YOUR INTERNAL COLLEAGUES AS CUSTOMERS — WITH THE SAME EYE TOWARD BRINGING THEM VALUE, FOR EXAMPLE — CAN HELP YOU BE MORE EFFICIENT AND EFFECTIVE."

Your company – Whom do you want to join the meeting?

Going to a meeting with other people from your company when you are meeting with more than one person is not only acceptable, it's good practice. It's always wise to have someone else who can help you stay on track, gauge interest levels, make sure that questions and objections (verbal and non-verbal) are addressed, and even take notes. Deciding on whom to bring (finance, marketing, HQ product, technical specialist, manager) can make a difference between closing a sale or not.

Defining your company's participants

 Complex B2B sales meetings

There are many factors in deciding who should join these meetings. Ultimately, choose people who can help you achieve your objective. There are many possibilities in this area when it comes to a Complex B2B sales process.

Customer account team

In most B2B solution sales there is an account team that is responsible for working with the customer. It usually consists of the sales person, the leader (for large customers there may be several sales people on the team), and at least one technical support person who is responsible for explaining how things work and understanding potential new solutions. Depending on the type of customer and/or opportunity, it could be a permanent team, an ad hoc team, or a virtual team. Whatever type, there should be a specific role for each participant at every meeting. The role could even be as an extra pair of ears. That may not sound like a critical role, but when you are speaking and/or managing a multi-person meeting, you cannot always pick up on all the nuances.

That said, there are times in the process when you specifically want to have a one-on-one meeting to gather particular information from the customer in an informal setting.

Defining your company's participants, cont.

HQ product visits

Usually, the HQ product people will have more detailed information, specifically about the roadmap and/or case stories from other customers and can bring value to the customer. Remember, though, that their agendas may be different from the account team's agenda.

Taking company executives to the customer

Most sales people I have met in Complex B2B sales processes have wanted help from executives, either to open doors or to show commitment. No matter the size of the company, executives cannot get to every customer, so the account team should use an executive customer visit strategically.

Sometimes an executive visit is planned by HQ to a territory for an internal meeting, or for some other reason not specifically related to the customer. Before deciding on creating a customer meeting, it would be wise to ask whether bringing an executive will aid or obstruct your objective. If you will need to escalate in the future, will an executive meeting today lower your ability to use that executive later? If you are trying to establish your credibility, will it help or hinder if you bring your boss from abroad? Is this executive someone who helps sales processes? Does the executive send the right message for the process? Will the executive suppress open discussion?

Having an executive visit too early in the process can lower local managers' positioning with the customer. On the other hand, it can show HQ commitment.

Defining your company's participants, cont.

 Internal meeting

Internal business meetings often include, for political reasons, people who feel they must contribute if they are there. The guideline here is first to define the role of each participant and see if there are other ways to give them information if the only reason they are joining is informative.

 Job interview/Request a raise

In a job interview, you depend on yourself. The only other people you bring with you, in a sense, are your references and how you choose to use them. With proper planning, you can mention different jobs or people to strengthen your case, as long as it does not descend from relevance to name-dropping.

The importance of internal alignment

At an executive meeting at a large telecom in South Africa, the senior executive from our company had flown in that morning and was quickly briefed by the local office manager. The rest of the team had been briefed separately on what we were presenting and how much time we had. Very little discussion was devoted to why we were presenting or to our ultimate goal.

At the meeting, the executive responsible for product from our company thought he was leading the meeting in the most appropriate direction, but he wasn't aware of the signals the others were sending, and wasn't in tune with the fact that he wasn't actually the leader of the meeting at all. He made promises and commitments that were impossible to deliver, setting up the rest of the team for failure. By doing so, he also undermined the senior sales executive and the local sales manager, who had set up a strategy of what they wanted to sell and deliver in the next 18 months.

Just because several people come from the same company does not mean everyone's objectives are aligned. In some companies, people do not even know each other. It doesn't matter how many people from your company are going to a meeting — you all need to be aligned and there must be a designated leader.

"It doesn't matter if there are two people or 15 from your company going to a meeting — you all need to be aligned and there must be a designated leader."

Creating alignment

 Complex B2B sales meeting

In a situation where multi-national companies are selling to multi-national companies and there are many players, the internal alignment of the team is so important that I give it its own mini-checklist.

Alignment checklist

- ☐ Define leader
- ☐ Verify everyone knows objectives
- ☐ Define and communicate leader signals
- ☐ Verify everyone knows everyone's role
- ☐ Set time for all to meet before meeting

1. Leader

Start with who is leading the meeting.

It seems obvious, but it's not. You may have someone joining who is very senior, but leading based on seniority is not always in the best interest of the meeting.

The person who has overall responsibility for organizing the meeting is also responsible for the checklist and for ensuring that the leader is defined. When you are the leader, you are responsible from the planning to the summary and action items. Even if during the meeting you pass the leadership to someone else for tactical reasons, you are still responsible for the entire meeting.

Creating alignment, cont.

2. Verify everyone knows objectives

During the preparation meeting, ensure that everyone knows what the overall objectives are and define when and how to pass the lead to someone else if things don't go as planned. If there is a large group presenting from different product divisions, the leader should see the presentation in advance to make sure there is nothing that can cannibalize the long-term objectives the account team has with the customer. The technical product person might be extremely knowledgeable, but also a little too direct and forthcoming with information. Does that person know to ask questions, pause, and not go into too much unnecessary detail?

3. Define and communicate leader signals

It's also a good idea to set up leader "cues" for when the leader will stop a question from being answered, slow someone down or speed them up, or give someone a three-minute warning to wrap up their presentation and leave time for questions.

4. Verify everyone knows everyone's role

This is especially important in a large meeting with many players, because it is very important that internal politics are not played out in front of the customer! When people understand their role and the role of others, they are more likely to be supportive of the cause versus unintentionally harming a situation.

Creating alignment, cont.

5. Set time for all to meet before meeting

Athletes have the benefit of brightly colored team uniforms so they don't pass the ball by mistake to the other side. Since business people do not color-coordinate their outfits, at least make sure before the main meeting that people from your company can recognize each other, and can tell each other apart from the customer. In multi-national companies where people don't even know each other, it's critical to meet face-to-face at least 15 minutes beforehand so that everyone knows who is on the home team.

Just recently a friend told me about a meeting with a large system integrator in Europe where he was representing a product line from the vendor's side. During the meeting, he had no idea who was from his company and who was from the customer's. Keep in mind that you will rarely have nametags or full control over seating arrangements.

 Internal meeting

When you are bringing people with you to help you make a point and achieve a specific agenda, they need to understand what is expected of them and why, and to agree to be part of the cause versus focusing on their own agenda. This is not always trivial, so proper preparation is needed to get people on board in advance.

Creating alignment, cont.

 Job interview/Request a raise

Since you are interviewing alone, the alignment is with yourself. Do you want this position? Do you believe you have something you can contribute to the company? What is unique about you? Do these questions resonate with you?

When you can answer these questions positively, you will be better aligned for your interview, and your body language and vocal tone will reflect the content of what you say.

Setting expectations

When it comes to business, we often like to think we are all on the same page — that we understand each other's goals, have common values and norms, and that we are mind readers and know each other's priorities and mindset.

This is especially true when we know the people and have a relationship with them. We tend to expect that this relationship will continue unchanged from the previous meeting, but it doesn't work like that.

For example, in a previous meeting you shared information about market trends and how they could affect the customer. The attendees were engaged and you had a good conversation. Now you set up another meeting where you will present a solution, but since then the customer has already met with your competitor or had different crises/priorities to deal with. As surprising at it may be, it's even possible that they don't remember that a second meeting has been arranged.

The best practice is to assume they do *not* remember your upcoming meeting, or that they will look at their agenda that morning and run into the meeting without remembering why you are having it. An email or call at the beginning of the week before the meeting and a short follow-up the day before is a great practice.

Reminders and setting expectations

 Complex B2B sales meeting

To help others come to the meeting in the right frame of mind, it helps to remind them beforehand of the meeting: why it's happening, what the agenda is, and what needs to be prepared. This also enables your contact to re-examine the attendance list and see if there are others who need to be there.

 Internal meeting

Send an agenda to all the people a day before and remind them of your objectives and why you have called this meeting. Assume they won't read details/presentations you have sent in advance.

 Job interview/Request a raise

Your best bet is to check online beforehand and see what is happening with the company you are interviewing with. Have there been any changes in ownership? Any news or press releases? Find out any information you can. If your company has just reported on a very bad financial quarter, you may want to reconsider asking for a raise right now.

Download the worksheet pack at http://www.dorisella.com/book
Password: 6STEPS

BUSINESS MEETINGS THAT WORK

Worksheet 2: People

Name of Customer _____ Date of Meeting _____

People

- ☐ Define and verify who attends (customer/external)
- ☐ Define and verify who is joining me (internal), and who will help me
- ☐ Verify internal alignment is complete
- ☐ Verify expectations with all attendees

Customer Attendees

Name	Title	Relationship
Mary Smith	Head of New Products	Score 3 – Have met before, but she is neither pro nor against. She is influential in the decision-making process.

Internal Attendees

Name	Title	Role in Meeting
Bob Smith	HQ Product Specialist	Technical representative of product Road Map and delivery times

Internal Alignment

Who is the leader? _____

- ☐ Verified everyone knows objectives
- ☐ Defined and communicated leader signals
- ☐ Verified everyone knows everyone's role
- ☐ Set time for all to meet before meeting

Expectations

- ☐ Meeting Objectives and Agenda sent to customer
- ☐ Google important attendees for changes in company

Copyright 2018 © | info@dorisella.com

STEP 3: STATE OF MIND

Everything we do reflects our mindset

As humans, we function from our State of Mind (SOM) — whether we are happy or sad, preoccupied or focused, curious or bored, trusting or skeptical, angry or pleased. Our SOM changes all the time. Sometimes we are conscious of the change and sometimes we realize it only with a physical symptom (like a headache). Think of those movies where the basketball player stands at the foul line, about to shoot the decisive point in the game. The crowd is going crazy! Suddenly there is SILENCE. The player focuses and shoots the ball in slow motion. He scores the winning point and the sound comes back in a roar!

That is what we call getting into the ultimate SOM to achieve your objective.

Our SOM affects the way we perceive things and our ability to listen without judgment. Just think of your SOM when you're going into an important meeting after getting a phone call from an angry customer. Not exactly the ultimate SOM, right?

I once got to a meeting in Romania with the CTO of ORANGE Telecom. As I was waiting for it to start, I realized I had misplaced my purse with my passport, credit cards, mobile phone, and all of my cash. I don't need to tell you that my ability to focus in that meeting was minimal. My SOM was far from optimal and I didn't get much from that meeting.

What is amazing is that when we know what SOM we want our customers to experience, and what SOM we need for ourselves, we can plan and manage it. With experience and practice, even in the most distracting situation, you can actually move yourself into your optimal, most productive SOM and make sure you do your utmost to achieve your objectives.

DEFINITIONS

State of Mind (SOM)

The concept of SOM refers to the mental and physical sense a person has at any given moment, as both are connected. SOM changes often and is dependent upon our interaction with the external world. It is a reflection of how we interpret a situation.

Attendees' SOM

Sales of any sort are always accompanied by a State of Mind. The SOM changes during the meeting — at least it should — and different people will be in different SOMs. Everything we do, and the way we do everything, reflects the current SOM.

For example, when you want to close a deal, it is much easier when you create a SOM of confidence and trust. You might start a meeting with attendees in a receptive SOM, but if you challenge them their SOM goes on the offensive. This is not necessarily negative, but you should be aware of it and make sure to recognize the offensive SOM. Some people may be in a skeptical SOM at the start of the meeting, but once you have convinced them, their SOM shifts and they can be the best people to help you sell your idea to other people in their organization, as they have already overcome their skeptical SOM. People who are annoyed, distrusting, bored, or lacking confidence are less likely to do business with you.

By including preparation for the SOM of your customers, you can more easily gauge the advancement of the meeting, know when it's right to introduce a topic, and have the flexibility to adjust your agenda throughout. If the SOM in the room is tense after many objections, it's probably not the time you want to introduce a problem you are facing or a price issue that may cause even more tension.

Let's focus on three distinct periods in the meeting to gauge attendee SOMs:

Expected SOM at the beginning of the meeting

I prefer to expect neutral at best, and skeptical or annoyed at worst. Even if attendees display curiosity, I prefer to plan for neutral and use my content to try to get them to even more "curious."

Desired SOM at the end of the meeting

Yes, you want them to be happy, curious, trusting, satisfied and excited. But being realistic can help you plan what you need to do next to honestly assess the situation and where you are in your sales process.

Expected SOMs while moving from the beginning of the meeting to end (A to B)

Planning for the changing SOMs, as your attendees move from the beginning of the meeting toward the end, gives top sales people maximum flexibility during the meeting to help shift SOMs along a continuum, or from point A to point B. First, it's a gauge: Once you are aware that there has been a shift in the SOM, you know you are going in the right direction. Let's say you are meeting with a customer who is almost convinced to go with a competitive solution. The initial SOM, when you present your solution, will probably be skeptical, perhaps with a bit of curiosity (they have taken the time to have a meeting with you, so you can infer that there is some interest). The desired end SOM would be intrigued and open to new ideas, doubting what they thought they knew and trusting that you have an idea seriously worth exploring. (Note that you are not expecting to officially close a deal in this situation.) During the meeting you will expect skepticism (if you don't, you won't be attuned to hearing potential objections and you will lose an opportunity to make a change), and perhaps anger (they haven't been given all the information, or they don't like being challenged with new information). You want to get them to a level of interest that shows they are moving toward a level of openness to new suggestions.

People don't move from A to B immediately; there is a process they need to go through that you can control with the content you bring to the meeting and by creating the rapport necessary for each stage. Understanding the customers' expected and desired SOM enables you to be flexible in controlling the meeting.

SOM continuum

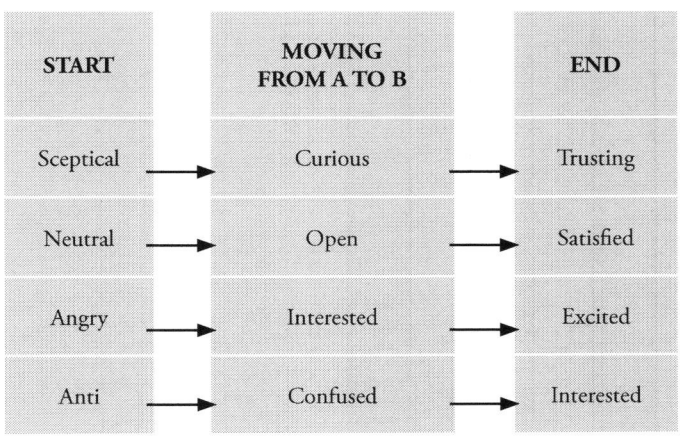

Personal SOM

Just as important, or perhaps the most important, is your own SOM — whether as the vendor or the leader of the meeting, or as an interviewee. When you know what your personal goal is for your optimal SOM, you can use different techniques to maintain it.

Just by being aware of your SOM, and where you want to be, is often enough to help regain control of a situation. Do you want to be assertive, confident, listening, knowledgeable, flexible, focused, and in control? Or do you walk into a meeting and let your SOM swing according to what happens?

Planning in advance for scenarios that might make you lose your desired SOM can help you maintain it when things inevitably occur to upset it. What happens to your SOM if the most important person you were expecting does not show up for your meeting? Or the room set-up is not what you had hoped, or people are coming and going — or, my favorite, the customer/interviewer is on the phone? You might show up for a meeting with what you thought was an agreed-upon agenda, only to find that your customer had a problem with a different department in your company and is upset at your company. The question is how to find and maintain your optimal SOM throughout the meeting. no matter what transpires.

Anchoring personal SOM

In the realm of personal SOM, there is something called an "anchor" — an action or movement that triggers awareness. All your senses are immediately reminded to get into a desired SOM.

Using anchors to remind yourself to get into your optimal meeting SOM is a great tool. A pilot recently told me that even before he starts his checklist, as soon as he walks into the cockpit and notices the anti-bacterial wipes used for cleaning the microphone (a simple addition that helps avoid so many illnesses), he gets into "pilot SOM". Merely seeing the wipes triggers the action of using them, and using them sets his brain in focus to be in "pilot SOM" and start the checklist. It's similar to musicians picking up their instruments before going on stage, or a sales person turning the phone to silent before a meeting. The wipes, the musical instruments, the action with the phone are all examples of SOM anchors.

Do this a few times to help you get into the optimal SOM. This should be practiced way before the meeting or directly after a great meeting.

Create an anchor for optimal "meeting leader" SOM

Take a few moments and remember a time you were at your best in a meeting. For me, it's having attributes like being focused, prepared, aware of my objective, knowledgeable on topic, in listening mode, confident, and feeling ready to deal with everything that comes along. You can choose and define your optimal SOM.

Once you can imagine that situation, take a deep breath and spend a few minutes remembering what it felt like; what you saw, heard and felt, or what you said to yourself at the time.

When the feeling is strong, "anchor" it by putting your thumb and forefinger together and breathing deeply or taking a step forward, or placing your hands on your stomach, or looking up … whatever feels most natural to you.

Then, every time you attend a meeting, repeat your anchor. Being in the optimal SOM is very important, and the anchoring process really works. Try it and send me feedback on how great it works for you.

Gauging shifts in SOM

The SOM of your colleagues in a meeting has an effect on you and on everyone in the room. If a colleague's body language reflects disagreement while you are making a point, it may throw you off and also send a message to the customer to question what you are saying. Even if the change in body language comes from having just read a disquieting text, once someone's SOM has changed, everyone in the meeting will pick up on it — even if not consciously. Like a yawn or a blush, SOM is infectious!

Everyone joining your meeting from your company needs to be 100 percent present in the meeting. If they need to take another call, they should walk out. Sitting with a customer and texting or reading email is not okay. It sends conflicting messages to the customer.

If your customers are doing that — texting while driving, so to speak — you will have to decide how you want to maintain your own SOM, and you have a great opportunity there to stop and get their attention back. Your team should be actively participating in the meeting by setting an example of a "listening" SOM, with full attention on the speaker. You should agree in advance with your team on this general mode of behavior.

You gauge SOM by asking questions and paying attention to non-verbal language when your get an answer. This can help you calibrate what is positive and what is negative.

There are many books and courses on personality types and body language. My concern is always that since most of us are not professionals at reading body language or analyzing personality types, we tend to make generalizations and fixate on hasty judgments.

In general, though, our non-verbal communication says a lot more than our verbal communication. Our senses know when we don't believe someone, even if we don't know why. It often means that there is a lack of calibration between the verbal and the nonverbal communication. For example, I have worked in two separate situations where certain colleagues put on huge, fake smiles whenever they were absolutely furious. Those smiles were a clear sign to beware!

Gauging change of SOM is an art that can be perfected simply by paying attention to the details. It's something we do naturally when we are in tune, as when we know that people are engaged or getting restless and bored. By making a list of the potential SOMs your attendees will experience during your meeting, you will be more likely to stay on top of this and be able to steer the meeting in the direction you desire.

"SINCE MOST OF US ARE NOT PROFESSIONALS AT READING BODY LANGUAGE OR ANALYZING PERSONALITY TYPES, WE TEND TO MAKE GENERALIZATIONS AND FIXATE ON HASTY JUDGMENTS."

Positive or Negative? Not that difficult to tell.

Being able to calibrate positive and negative reactions is the key to success for anyone in any type of sales, whether you are selling a product, an idea, or yourself. It usually happens naturally, without even thinking about it. Pre-meeting small talk enables an observant sales person to identify and absorb the customer's positive and negative reactions through head movement, body gestures, and minute facial movements around the eyes and lips. These preliminary observations will help identify changes in SOM and when an objection has been overcome.

> Note: Beware of "universal" body language interpretations. People can cross their arms to connote defensiveness or a closing of the mind, certainly. But they also do it when they are cold or tired, or when they are not fully understanding, or when they just remembered they forgot to feed the dog.

Gauge SOM

Watch

Watch for changes in body language, which indicate a change of SOM. Having more than one person with you in the meeting can help you read the signs. When someone suddenly moves and makes a major shift in body language, a change of SOM is also happening.

Listen

Listen for changes in tone of voice. When people are nervous or excited, their voices go up. Excitement can be a good thing, so be careful not to judge without first considering the context of what is being said.

Listen

Listen for the questions and language people use. Have they started to ask more questions about how they can use your solution, versus merely raising objections?

If time is short

Rule of thumb for when you only have 30 seconds to prepare:

- Clarify your Objective
- Check your personal SOM

Download the worksheet pack at http://www.dorisella.com/book
Password: 6STEPS

BUSINESS MEETINGS THAT WORK

Worksheet 3: State Of Mind (SOM)

Name of Customer _____ Date of Meeting _____

State of Mind
- ☐ Define expected and desired SOM (attendees)
- ☐ Define and evaluate my desired personal SOM to maintain control of meeting
- ☐ Review SOM with other attendees
- ☐ Review ways to gauge movement from SOM to SOM

Attendees State of Mind
1. Expected at Beginning _____
2. Desired at End _____
3. Expected SOMs on way from A to B _____

Personal State of Mind
What attributes do I want to have for my ultimate SOM during the meeting?
1. _____
2. _____
3. _____

What could make me lose my ultimate SOM?
1. _____
2. _____
3. _____

Other Attendees' SOM
What are the attributes that are important for the teams' SOM?
1. _____
2. _____
3. _____

Copyright 2018 © | info@dorisella.com

STEP 4: CONTENT

The what and how of achieving objectives

So far we have discussed the Why of the meeting and Who are the people, and the SOM we expect and want. Now it is time for the What and the How. What should be the core content of the meeting? How should it be delivered?

You might be familiar with the 7 percent rule, from Albert Mehrabian's 1971 book *Silent Messages*. He asserted that in any situation, people pay attention, or more important — perceive a message based on only 7 percent actual content and 93 percent on how it's delivered (55 percent body language, 38 percent tone of voice). Even though there is healthy debate over the accuracy and validity of this study, anyone who has ever listened to someone speak knows that how the message is delivered is at least equally important as the content.

In this chapter we will look at some guidelines to help you both plan the content and its delivery. The assumption in this planning is that you have an objective for the specific meeting, and also know your long-range vision as well as the medium-range objective that will enable you to navigate the content of the meeting and be flexible as needed.

There are many ways to look at how to plan the content and its delivery. I have chosen four topics: Time, Main Points, Rapport, and Frames. These topics are generic enough to be appropriate for all types of business meetings — a phone call, a web meeting, a one-on-one, and a multi-attendee meeting. You might only have 5-10 minutes beforehand to go over the content checklist and pick and choose what is most important to help you achieve your objectives. You will find when you start putting your content onto the worksheet, that any part of the checklist can be as deep as you need in order to get results from even the most complex of meetings.

DEFINITIONS

Rapport
Basic chemistry between people that creates trust and understanding. It is the ability to see the other's point of view and get others to understand yours.

Content
The core subject and material you will be discussing.

Story
What story will you tell, using your content, so it is both relevant and understood by your audience.

Story frames
A term used to create the context, focus, or guidance that we want the listener to use when processing the content.

Time – What does it mean?

Time is one of the most valued commodities in this busy world. As such, it should be honored.

Time also has different meanings in different cultures. It goes beyond "being on time," or what hour a meeting is supposed to start or end. Just as important is planning the use of time in the meeting.

I highly recommend you get to know the culture in which you are working, especially on its time-related customs. There are many excellent books and resources for getting familiar with cultural issues.

Here are some examples of how time works in different cultures:

- In Southeast Asia you need to establish a long-term relationship with people with whom you work, one of the many reasons large companies rely on local representatives.
- Western cultures working in China all tell stories of protracted small talk and delays until the very last minute before critical issues are raised, particularly when they have a flight to catch. Experienced sales people know to have the alternative of catching a later flight.
- In Southern Europe it is common to drink alcohol at lunch before an afternoon meeting. Getting important business done early is usually good practice.

There are cultures where people are always late, and others where they are always punctual. Make it a point to always be punctual while also respecting local customs.

For all cultures, it is sound business to set expectations for how much time is available for the meeting and whether specific people will only be available for a limited time. (I always re-check this at the beginning of the actual meeting.)

> **Warning!**
> **Knowing how much time is available**
>
> Knowing how much time is available helps you plan the content and the questions. It ensures that you get your main points across before "running out of time."
>
> I often hear sales people say, "They were so interested that they stayed another hour." In general, though, no one likes being kept late. Don't be surprised if people just get up and go when you are not respectful of their time.

Time planning

Stay focused on your objectives, not the content

You will rarely be able to say everything you want to say in the way you want, but in your planning leave time for what will most help you achieve your objectives. When you know in advance what is most important, you have the ability to make changes during the meeting.

Prioritize your topics

Start with the most important, and allocate time accordingly. At the same time, you may need to plan the topics differently in order to establish rapport and get a good story. Prior prioritization gives you the flexibility to make changes during the meeting if you need to spend more time on one topic.

Leave time for questions and discussion

People absorb more when they have an opportunity to discuss and ask questions. Later we will review how to prepare the content to enable discussion and not leave a void.

Content is more than just a presentation

Whether you are going to a sales meeting or a job interview, or having an internal meeting or a board meeting, you most likely have some idea of the content you already have, or will use to present or discuss. There is no need to reinvent the wheel each time. However, to maximize success, you will want to tailor your content or story to the specific audience, to match the objective and the expected initial SOM and the desired ending SOM. (Tailoring includes deleting of logos of your customer's competition from your slides or document. Or removing another company's name from your cover letter for a job application.)

In every sales-oriented meeting, even when the topic is technical specification of how something works, **there is an underlying goal to get the listener/customer engaged and in discussion**. Otherwise you don't need to have a meeting at all.

I am sure you know this, yet I still see many times where a sales or technical sales person dominates the conversation or spends the majority of the time presenting too many slides with a narrow goal of simply finishing the presentation. It is similar to an interview where the interviewee does not stop to ask questions. If you have ever been in any type of organization, you have encountered people who dominate the meeting and do not allow for discussion or sharing; invariably, many people turn to their phones.

Here is a list of questions to guide you in defining the content that will help achieve your objectives:

- What is the base content that will best help achieve objectives?

- Where is the customer in the sales cycle? Do they need to be convinced of something, or do they want more information about what you are offering or how it works? Do they want to know why they should trust you?
- What other information (trends, case studies, etc.) can you share that will create interest and develop a discussion?
- What specifically does your audience need to know and what do they *not* need to know in order to achieve your objective?
- What do they *already* know?

> **Warning! What do they know?**
>
> I once participated in a meeting where the sales rep went into a long, involved explanation of a new technology standard that was being used in the market. For the first eight to ten minutes the customer was polite, even though it was clear they were not interested. Eventually the senior person said to the sales person, "Do you really think we are not aware of this technology and that we need you to teach us what it is? Tell us what solutions you have and let's move on."
>
> Lessons learned:
>
> 1. Be prepared to explain and set the stage, but ask before you start going into "teaching the obvious".
> 2. Pay attention to the customer's non-verbal language (boredom, frustration).
> 3. Be flexible and able to pivot away if something isn't working.

Define content

HERE ARE SOME EXAMPLES OF how you would use these questions to create the content for your meeting:

 Complex B2B sales meeting

Base content

Solution that best fits customer needs (or something new you want to introduce).

Create interest

Present market trends/Use Cases pertaining to solution.

What they need to know

Depending on the stage, they first need to know how it will help them before getting into "how does it work".

What they already know

This is especially important when you are talking about topics to which you have a strong personal attachment. Sometimes listeners (if they can get a word in edgewise) will say, '"I'm aware of that, but tell me what is unique about what you have." More often, you will just lose the attendees' attention by going into detail about how it works and not getting to the point of how it brings value.

Define content, cont.

 **Internal meeting**

As a general rule, any repeating internal meeting should include the status of action items from the previous meeting.

Base content

Whatever topic needs to be discussed.

Create interest

Why is this relevant to everyone in the room, why must the priorities be changed, how it will benefit the bigger picture, etc.?

What they need to know

What must you share to help make a decision, and what can be sent before or after the meeting for more detailed information?

What they already know

If relevant, repeat the action items from the previous meeting to remind everyone. If it's a new topic, at least make sure everyone is on the same page.

Define content, cont.

 Job interview/Request a raise

Once you have scored an interview, whether it's face-to-face or via phone/web, being prepared with the content can mean the difference between getting the job or the raise or not.

Base content

How can you bring value to the job based on your experience and their job description?

Create interest

Prepare in advance actual stories of what you have done so that you are ready with them and can give examples.

What they need to know

Only what is relevant to the job or specifically asked. You are moving on to something new, and do not need to relate everything that happened with a boss you hated. However, if there is something that is critical for you in your working environment (such as working independently and not liking a hands-on boss), by all means share it. You want to make sure this position is right for you.

What they already know

If you have come from a different industry, be careful when you use jargon to explain what you have done before. You may need to give a concise overview of your previous industry and how things worked there.

Asking questions to develop discussion

The best way to open a discussion is to **ask questions** and **listen for the answers**. I can't begin to calculate the number of times I have heard great questions, only to have the answer interrupted by the asker.

Questions get people engaged and they give you information. Asking questions is important in any type of meeting. The best questions are about business issues, decision motivation, needs, and desires. When you prepare your questions, be careful not to focus on information you could have found out in advance. It's okay to bring information and ask to verify it; this shows that you have done your homework, and also enables you to open a deeper discussion. There are many good books on asking questions. For Complex B2B meetings, I recommend taking a look at SPIN™ and the CHALLENGER™ for best practices on asking questions.

PRACTICAL USE

Sample discussion questions

 Complex B2B sales meetings

- These are the market trends in your region. Are you seeing the same trends in your country? How does that affect your business?
- What are the main subjects you are focusing on in the next 12-18 months in order to achieve your business objectives?
- How do you see yourself resolving [a particular] problem?
- Assuming you are interested in this [proposal/topic/solution], what steps do we need to go through?
- Is there any reason we cannot move forward on this in the next two weeks?

 Internal meeting

- In what way have you experienced …(whatever the problem may be)?
- How did you overcome the problem?
- What ideas do you have?

PRACTICAL USE

Sample discussion questions, cont.

 Job interview

- I read that the industry is facing (certain challenges), how does this effect your company?
- What do you see as the major challenges for the person in this position?

Asking listeners for questions — When is the best time?

Sometimes people like to wait until the end of a presentation before taking questions. This is a mistake, unless you are in a room with more than 30 people.

Once you finish your presentation, you are in effect lowering the curtain. Your audience will be in a different SOM, like at a theater when the audience stands and is ready to go home. Your audience knows that you have come to the end, and instead of spontaneously asking questions they are more likely to be guarded.

Even if they do offer questions, those questions are likely to be more controlled. The information you receive will not be as "clean" as when questions and objections arise naturally during discussion.

Creating rapport: The HOW of getting your message across

Rapport (chemistry) with your audience — whether it is an audience of one or a thousand — is basic to being able to get your message across. This is just as important if you are meeting with people you know well and even consider good friends, or with people you've never met before.

When there are people with whom you do not get along or with whom you have a conflict, it's a good idea to pay special attention to creating rapport. Sales people do this instinctively with stories and small talk before the meeting. Sharing common hobbies (golf, football, music), or talking about traffic or any non-confrontational topic is usually a safe way to create initial rapport.

Rapport is a combination of science and art. The science refers to the guidelines, provided below, which include how to prepare in advance for situations where you know you may have difficulty creating rapport. The art is in knowing when and how to use it, all of which comes with practice.

There are many ways to create and maintain rapport in a meeting. One of the ways is the pre-meeting small talk. Most experienced sales people who are masters of small talk are not only "making conversation"; they are actively gathering important information, including non-verbal cues. There is also a lot of information available on how to create physical rapport by matching and mirroring your customer's physical movements.

Here I focus on a few ways of planning to create rapport, based on content, that are especially helpful when you know you are likely facing a difficult situation. By preparing in advance and knowing what you will do if rapport is broken, you can quickly re-set the meeting and re-establish rapport using some of the tips below.

Rapport makes a difference

I was at a major telecom operator in Moscow, meeting with the Chief Technical Officer (CTO). The senior sales VP from my company had specifically requested I come to this meeting to discuss the business rationale behind the solutions we had in our portfolio.

Regardless of the cultural and language differences, it was apparent after just three minutes that I would not be able to check the box for rapport, or relevant content. What I had to say obviously held no interest for him.

I checked with him and he told me that he was already convinced of the business case for these solutions. What he wanted was more information on how the solution worked, which was out of my realm of expertise.

Fortunately, my colleague — who had technical know-how on how it worked — was in a nearby room in a different meeting. I quickly went to get him and we switched places, as the meeting with the CTO was more important. The customer appreciated the flexibility and our ability to quickly adjust the agenda, and this enabled us to continue in the sales process and win some 'relationship' points.

Setting expectations to create rapport

One of the first ways to establish rapport at the beginning of a meeting is to set expectations. What will we be doing? How long do we have? Will the format be interactive or a formal presentation with Q&A?

In addition to establishing rapport, setting expectations also helps you gauge the SOM of the audience, giving you the flexibility to make adjustments accordingly. If you lose rapport during the meeting, stopping and re-setting expectations can help re-establish the rapport.

Establish rapport by setting expectations

Time

"We are set to meet until X (time) and I want to make sure that is still correct."

Meeting Objective (This is not necessarily your objective, but the topic for the meeting.)

You will most likely start by reminding them of your last meeting and set the stage for this one by backtracking (going over what you did at the last meeting). Discussing what was done the last time or up until now helps everyone remember the context of the discussion and helps sidestep misunderstandings, which can diminish rapport.

People

"Will X be joining us? Is there anyone else who should be here?" This is important after the objective has been reviewed, as people will often ask others to join, or you may find that you have the wrong people in the room (this has happened to me).

Mode of meeting

What will be the mode or the format of the meeting? Is there an expectation that it will be interactive, with the sharing of ideas? How long will you allot for each section? Or, do you prefer to have a presentation before the discussion? When you prepare, think of what will best achieve your objectives, and not just what makes you most comfortable. For example, you might prefer to present before taking questions, but you might get more information if the meeting is wholly interactive.

> **Late arrivals**
>
> Acknowledge those who come late to a meeting and give them the context of your discussion as soon as you can. If the person is critical to your objectives, repeat the main points.

The power of stories to create rapport

Stories are loved by all — especially when they are relevant to the listener. Most people also enjoy personal stories, with the level of detail depending on the audience.

Stories are a great way to create curiosity. They use metaphors that describe the issue you will be discussing later. Stories are also powerful for creating rapport and changing SOM, especially if you know ahead of time that your audience may not be in the best initial SOM for you to achieve your objective.

In everyday conversation we tell stories and don't usually plan why we are telling them, but stories used in meetings are best when they have a purpose. They are not just for the sake of talking. When we are connected to our objective and focused on the audience, stories will tend to be relevant and come naturally, as opposed to when we are focused on our stories and ourselves. The best practice is always to be focused on the listener and attuned to non-verbal language and change of SOM while you are speaking.

You can use the small-talk session, before anyone sits down, to tell stories. You can even use stories as you actually begin the meeting; "Before we get started, I wanted to share…"

With a story, you can first establish rapport by acknowledging a situation with a metaphor so as not to be too direct, and then continue to lead the audience to the desired SOM.

One of the most difficult situations I was in was when I had to open a session at an international conference the morning after the attacks on the World Trade Center. There were many people present from different cultures, yet I had to create rapport with everyone and also change the SOM (shock, total lack of interest in the topic) to one of curiosity and at least some level of attentiveness.

I was concerned with what I would say and how I would open the morning and spent quite a bit of time planning. I decided that instead of opening with, "We are all in a state of shock," I would say, "Many of us are in a state of shock and have been closely following the news since yesterday." Saying "many of us" versus "all of us" was to make sure that everyone in the room was included, even those who were not following the news.

I then suggested we take a few moments of silence, before continuing with, "We have all come here today to learn about [the topic], so despite the fact that many of us sitting in this room are not 100 percent mentally present, I want to ask all of you a question. How many of you have ever experienced . . .?" From there, I led them into the discussion topic.

In this situation, the "story" was simply enabling each person, in a moment of silence, to tell their own story to themselves, and at the same time I was ready to lead them in the direction I wanted to take them: the topic of the meeting.

Usually, you will have situations where even a simple story can do wonders. When you know that there may be certain negative SOMs, such as lack of trust in the ability of your solution to work in their environment, you can say: "Before we get started, I wanted to share with you that last week I talked to a customer similar to you who had been very skeptical about the ability to implement [solution]; however, they said that they decided to go ahead anyway because [xyz]." There is no need to mention names of customers, but by giving a reference you can lower objections and bring up sensitive issues in advance that you know will be difficult to discuss later.

Stories make a difference

A sales executive was preparing for a meeting with a group of executives from his company at the site of an important customer. He knew the customer had already made some purchasing decisions that did not include his company. His goal in the meeting was to create doubt in their decision by bringing new information about the long-term benefits his solution could provide.

The person who was going to be presenting the new information was a brilliant young product expert. He knew that the initial SOM in the room would be skeptical and closed, and that the only reason the customer had agreed to meet was out of respect for a senior executive from the selling company who would be present.

During our planning, we were looking for a way to create an open or at least a neutral SOM before the meeting. The plan was to tell a story that would be relevant, while also leaving a metaphorical message.

The sales exec began his story after the introductions. "Before we get started, I'm curious to know if any of you got stuck on the highway in the last week." (He knew that 99 percent of them would have gotten stuck on the highway due to recent flooding.) "I got stuck today for the fourth time this week and I heard a very interesting story about how the government plans to resolve the problem of flooding on the highway," he continued. "I don't know if you are aware, but there have been many long meetings by all the top experts on how to solve the problem of the flooding. They even brought in experts from abroad and spent thousands of dollars on different solutions. Last month, a university student presented a brilliant idea he had recently come up with. After a few weeks of testing, it's clear that this idea, which no one had thought of before, will resolve the flooding issue for good. Amazing, isn't it? Reminded me of the story of the little Dutch boy and the hole in the dyke."

This is subliminal, but when people hear a story they are more likely to lower resistance and be open to hear what the young product manager has to say, and perhaps to changing their decision.

Creating stories

1. What is the main message you want to get across? Think in terms of abstract ideas: create an openness to hear a new idea, lower skepticism or even frustration with your company, create curiosity.

2. Think of examples for "openness" or skepticism or frustration. Use a thesaurus to think of metaphors, or Google the words and look for images to help get ideas for story-creating metaphors:

   Openness: Honesty, directness, frankness, sincerity, candidness. Pictures of door opening, peeking through a keyhole, hands open above you.

   Skepticism: Cynicism, disbelief, doubt, uncertainty, suspicion, distrust. Pictures of Pinocchio, politicians.

3. Plan your story so that it connects to your overall topic (yes, this takes practice). Listen to stories other people around you tell and see what works for you. What feels right? What sounds right?

4. Google metaphors for the word you want, looking for great stories online that you can adapt.

Warning! Do not tell a story that doesn't make sense to you or sound right. Your authenticity is THE most important thing.

Creating stories, cont.

5. Leave jokes for social gatherings unless you know your audience very well, or unless telling a joke is part of your content and style. Sense of humor is cultural and very personal. It's fine to laugh at yourself and be known for your great sense of humor, but don't plan jokes or funny stories as part of your meeting story unless the story has no meaning and purpose without it. Your sales meetings are not the time to play toastmaster.

Frames: Giving context to content

Have you ever heard someone start telling you a story and after a few minutes you say, "Hold on — what are you talking about? What is this in reference to?" Frames help set the context in which we want someone to listen to us. What is the overall topic and what are we specifically discussing at the moment? Common frames that I'm sure you've all heard of include "What we will do today" and "In summary."

I cannot count the number of meetings I have attended where it is clear that people are talking about completely different things. This happens in one-on-one meetings and group meetings. One of the most common frame mistakes has to do with point of view. When you say "you will benefit," who is "you," exactly? Is it "you" as end user, consumer, partner working with "us" on a deal? You as investor? As the person doing the hiring?

Usually, when we realize that we are not on the same page with our audience and have lost rapport, we instinctually create a frame. However, this recognition often comes with tension and negative SOM that can easily be avoided.

Frames need to be set and reset during meetings, especially with complex topics where you always want to remind everyone of the big picture and of where you are now. You may even need to stop and remind everyone why you are discussing the topic in the first place.

PRACTICAL USE

Frames and how they are used

Pre-Framing

It is used for getting a message across before you start the real discussion. The use of this is very powerful. When discussion begins, participants are usually in a "listening" SOM that may also include a "skeptical" or "objection" SOM. In the ***Before Frame***, you have an opportunity to tell a story or use a metaphor that will lower future objections before the listener has the opportunity to go into an unwanted SOM. This is not a conscious action, but when used skillfully is very powerful. The simplest use is "Before we begin…"

Outcome frame

This is used to clarify expectations and focus attention. Most people use this instinctively with sentences like: "What we will do today/now" or "Our agenda is…"

Backtrack frame

To remind your audience where you are or what you discussed last time you met. Very useful for getting everyone on the same page, especially if someone joins late or after a break. Examples: "Last time we met we discussed…" "Up to now, we have been talking about…"

PRACTICAL USE

Frames and how they are used, cont.

"As If" frame

The main use is to make the topic relevant to listeners, *as if* they already agree with you or are using your solution. Give examples as if you had already made a decision, so the listener better connects to the topic. It is used in different ways in many sales situations, the most common being showing a demo: "If you were using it, it would help you…" "If we can suppose you have a budget, how could you use this?" And, in a job interview, "When I'm working here, I will . . ."

Open frame

Shows your audience that you want them to give input to open discussion with questions such as, "What do you think about this?" "When have you had similar issues?" "Any questions?" (For that last one, use the question in conversation. Do not make a slide that says "Questions?" Make your summary slide your last slide and ask for questions.)

Download the worksheet pack at http://www.dorisella.com/book
Password: 6STEPS

BUSINESS MEETINGS THAT WORK

Worksheet 4: Content

Name of Customer _____ Date of Meeting _____

Content
- ☐ Review time constraints
- ☐ Define main points to be covered
- ☐ Define your questions
- ☐ Define ways to create and maintain rapport
- ☐ Develop Story Frames

How much time is allocated for meeting? _____

Main Points to be covered /what percentage of time do I want for each topic/stage/Q&A?

Topic	Time	Presenter

Questions: What questions do I want to ask that will help move forward in the process?
_____
_____

Creating Rapport

What is the initial SOM that is expected and what is the SOM I want at the start of the meeting?
_____

What type of story can I tell or metaphors I can use to move others from SOM to SOM?
_____

Using Frames (Use the examples below to prepare your frames.)

Frame	
Pre-Framing	At the beginning: "Before we get started..."
Outcome Frame	Beginning: "What we will do today is...."
Backtrack Frame	Reminder re: last time, or before a new topic: "Up to now we have been discussing..." "Last meeting we discussed..."
As-if Frame	Demo/example of how to use the solution/idea, how it would work
Open Frame	A question after each topic: "Is this clear? Any questions? How would you use this...?"

Copyright 2018 © | info@dorisella.com

STEP 5: OBJECTIONS

An integral part of the sales process

People have different agendas and companies have different priorities. It is normal and even vital to hear objections and experience conflict during business meetings, as this is often the fuel for creativity and moving forward.

As a sales person or a leader of a business meeting, it is your job to anticipate and deal with objections and conflicts in the best way possible. The first step is to accept that objections and conflicts are inevitable, which will help you to prepare your responses and plan the SOM you want to be in when you hear those objections.

This chapter will discuss how to define potential objections and responses in advance, how to use stories and questions to open a discussion, and how to hear objections when you are not getting the information you need. As a bonus, I have added a guide to language patterns that can help you in your preparations.

> **DEFINITIONS**
>
> **Objection**
>
> As meeting participants consider the product, solution, service or issue you want to sell, they will invariably stumble over something that is not clear, or with which they do not agree, and they will express this in what may seem like disapproval or opposition.
>
> **Language patterns**
>
> Patterns of speech that reveal the underlying or deeper meaning of what a person is actually trying to say. When we understand the use of these filters, and how they are used in patterns of speech — especially when we hear objections — we are better equipped to clarify the objection and to respond to it.

Planning for objections

Objections are not just about what someone thinks is wrong with what you have said or presented. People need to understand ideas in their own terms. In the process of understanding, they will most likely express objections. If there have been *no* objections, perhaps you have not given them enough information or impetus to give true consideration to what you are offering.

There are many reasons you may hear objections. Your listeners might find your idea excellent and exciting, but at the same time know that there is no way for them to continue to sell it within their organization for reasons that are not necessarily tied to you or what you are offering. It could be related to company culture, executive preference for another vendor, previous investments gone wrong, pressure from the board to cut costs, etc.

Everyone reacts differently to objections. It depends of course on how the objections are presented, the tone of voice in which we hear them, and our own personal SOM at the moment. We also need to be aware of the trigger points on which the objection sits. What will make you lose your optimal SOM? This is especially tricky if you are challenged regarding a solution/idea in which you have a personal stake, or at a job interview where your integrity and professionalism are seemingly questioned.

The timing of objections is important as well. Your customer may use objections as a negotiation tactic and mention them just as you are ready to close. The more experience and knowledge you have, the more you know what objections to expect and the better prepared you can be.

To get attendees to raise objections, you can get help from other people and create a pre-planned role-play during the meeting with your colleagues or even with an internal champion. It could be with a prepared question that is launched at a certain time, or with a handy case study waiting in the wings for a particular, expected objection.

Listen!

I have sat in on many meetings where the sales person ignored or belittled objections. ANY objection you hear, no matter from whom, is valuable information about the way you are explaining something or how that explanation is being interpreted. Do not ignore any objections!

Preparing for possible objections

- Make a list in advance of every objection you have heard in the past and ask colleagues, too.
- If the topic is new and you can't think of what objections there might be, ask other people for their objections. Listen before trying to craft a response.
- Read market trends on what people are saying about the topic, including negative reports.
- Practice saying thank you (aloud or to yourself) when you hear a new objection. The objection gives you information and helps you do better next time.
- Prepare an internal FAQ with answers to help you, and share with your colleagues later.
- If you cannot respond on the spot, promise to get back to those with objections, and make sure you get back to them when you promised.

Preparing for NO objections

If we agree that objections are an important part of a sales process, then it would be wise to prepare for when you do not receive any objections. The reason you may not hear objections depends on both the culture and the situation.

- In Asia, generally speaking, if the senior person hasn't raised an objection, other people might not be comfortable doing so either.
- You may not have established the rapport necessary for the other person to feel comfortable raising objections.
- If what you have said remains unclear, it can be difficult to form objections.
- They simply may not be interested and want the meeting to end.
- There is the rare occasion when everyone is totally on board, but I would be wary before assuming this. The rule of thumb is that if it sounds too good, it usually is.

What you can do

- Ask questions that will open the door to objections. This enables you to get more information about what is going on in the mind of the person to whom you are selling.
- Give Use Cases and share other customers' initial objections and thoughts, including how they overcame them.

Bonus: Using language patterns to deal with objections

Language patterns are a powerful tool for gaining better understanding of what people mean when they say something. It is also a powerful tool for breaking down objections. In this bonus section we will review some basic language patterns that can provide another tool for dealing with objections.

One of the keys to dealing with objections is first to clarify what, exactly, is the objection. To what does it refer, and in what context? Is the objection because they really do not agree with you and have contrary information, or because they don't understand what you said? Is it general, or is it specific to a certain case?

Just as important is listening to the pattern of communication that the speaker uses. This gives you a better idea of how to answer beyond just the content of the objection, and also of the way the person is interpreting what you say.

Does this sound complicated? Don't worry — you already do this without thinking. Let's take a look at what you do intuitively when you are at your best at answering objections.

When analyzing patterns of communication, the famed linguist and philosopher Noam Chomsky (also a cognitive scientist, historian, social critic, and political activist) refers to three main filters in our minds that we use to help us absorb and communicate what we internalize from our senses, and how we then react.

These three filters are beneficial, though at times they limit our point of view and do not enable us to absorb, see, or hear the entire picture.

When we understand the use of these filters or patterns

of speech in everyday language — especially when we hear objections — we are better equipped first to clarify the objection and then to respond to it.

The three main filters that define how our brain processes the multitude of information it receives through our senses are Deletion, Distortion, and Generalization. Each has a pro and a con, depending on the situation. All three are used all the time, but sometimes one is dominant.

Let's take a look at these three filters and how they can be used to help overcome objections.

Dealing with deletion-based objections

A deletion-based objection is when the customer deletes important information that could change the meaning of the communication. A common deletion-based objection you may hear from a potential customer might be: "We don't have a budget."

Here, the speaker has omitted to tell us:

- What he doesn't have a budget for
- The time frame for this lack of budget
- What he *does* have a budget for
- Who else in the organization may have a budget

Potential Questions you could ask of this person:

- What exactly don't you have a budget for?
- When will your budget open?

- What types of things do you have a budget for?
- Is there anyone else who could benefit who does have a budget?

This may sound simplistic, but when you start breaking down objections and figuring out what information the speaker has "deleted," you have a better understanding of the scope of the objection and more flexibility in your response.

Another common deletion-based example is when someone says: "I'm not sure." Here, the speaker has omitted to say what exactly he is not sure about.

When we hear this type of objection, we also have filters and often assume or fill in what has not been said — and we are not always correct. You can follow up and ask the speaker: "What exactly are you not sure about?"

A good practice when preparing for a multi-person meeting is to designate someone who is also listening for at least one type of objection so that they can help you, as the leader of the meeting, to understand, answer, and break down objections in the best manner possible.

Dealing with distortion-based objections

A distortion-based objection is when speakers "distort" what they are saying by making a claim that A = B when there is not necessarily a factual connection between the two. A common distortion-based objection you may hear: "We can't be a valued customer if you can't provide [whatever it is] in time for our launch."

In this situation, the speaker is taking two experiences and interpreting them as synonymous. In most situations, they are not synonymous. Being a valued customer does not necessarily equal having something in time for a launch.

In this situation, the customer is mostly concerned that you won't be able to provide a solution on time, and you need to be sensitive to that. First you need to create rapport and deal with the stated problem. Only then can you work on breaking down the connection between A and B and focusing on the issue that needs to be resolved.

> **Step 1: Create rapport**: "The launch is next month [emphasize the short time]. Will you need the full solution by then? Could we find an interim solution?"
>
> **Step 2: Break the connection between A and B**: You can even ask questions that use the same distortion pattern: "We have done A, and that means B, which benefits you." "In the past we managed to deliver your needs within the time frame and even provide you with extra XXX. What other ways would you like us to show you that we value your business?"

Here's another distortion-based example, this one for a job interview, when the interviewer says: "It looks from your experience like you have only managed small groups; what makes you think you are prepared to manage larger groups?"

In this case, A ("only managed small groups") = B ("cannot manage large groups").

First of all, expect a question like that if you are interviewing for a position that is an upgrade for you. Since this is an interview, your response will be a bit different. You might think, but not say aloud: "Do you know any managers of large groups that started off managing smaller groups?"

Your objective here is to break the connection between small groups and large groups, and to do that you will start by creating rapport: "Of course there are differences between large groups and small groups. There are also some basic managerial skills that are important for both, wouldn't you agree?" List them, and continue to mention your proven skills.

The most important point is to be prepared for these types of questions so that when they arrive, you have the flexibility to respond while maintaining your optimal SOM.

Dealing with generalization-based objections

A generalization-based objection is just like it sounds — one that is all encompassing. It usually has the words "always" and/or "never," as in: "You always promise that you will deliver on time and you never do."

Dealing with generalizations is something we usually do intuitively when we hear such words as all, every, everyone, nobody, and never.

The initial response is as simple as just repeating the generalization. In the case above, I would probably put the emphasis on the negative, and say, "Never deliver on time?" Or, if I really never do, perhaps I would widen it to: "Perhaps we didn't deliver on the exact date we originally said, but was it on time for what it was needed for, with all the changes you requested?"

In this example, I have assumed that the generalization is also deleting information and I have added it back: "with all the changes you requested," and "it was on time for the changed due date."

If you are in the habit of promising things you cannot deliver, that is a different topic.

PRACTICAL USE

Language patterns

TYPE	PRO	CON
DELETION	Critical to enabling us to absorb anything and focus	Deleting important information limits our point of view
DISTORTION	Enables creatiity	Creates distorted view of a situation that can get you stuck
GENERALIZATIONS	Enables learning and can help understanding	Can create biases and limiting belief structures

Checklists are about reminding you to be aware of things you already know. You intuitively know how to answer people when you hear objections. The Checklist item on preparing for Language Patterns is just to remind you and give you another tool for achieving your objective. These Language Patterns have both positive and negative uses, and depend both on the context in which they are used and whether they benefit the speaker at that time.

Download the worksheet pack at http://www.dorisella.com/book
Password: 6STEPS

BUSINESS MEETINGS THAT WORK

Worksheet 5: Objections

Name of Customer _____ Date of Meeting _____

Objections

- ☐ Define potential objections and craft answers
- ☐ Create questions/stories to help hear objections
- ☐ Review language patterns to prepare for objections

Potential Objections and Responses

Objection	Response

Critical objections to raise if they have not been discussed:

1. _____
2. _____

Language Patterns *(Use the examples below to prepare and be ready to listen for language patterns.)*

	Listening Keys	Potential Objection Statements
Deletion	*Statements with no specific reference*	*They say your prices are high*
Distortion	*Because of A, B must be true*	*You didn't deliver on time last time, so they can't trust you*
Generalization	*Everyone, no one, always, never, every*	*Everyone knows it's true*

Copyright 2018 © | info@dorisella.com

STEP 6: CLOSING

It can be the most important part of a meeting

Have you ever participated in a meeting where people get up and start leaving before you have had time to discuss an important issue that came up near the end? Often there will be promises to follow up by email or to pick it up again "next time."

Closing a meeting is, in many ways, the most important part. It is the gauge as to whether you have achieved your objective. With that in mind, it is surprising how little forethought is usually given the close: who will do it, what will happen, how much time to leave for it.

In this chapter we discuss ways to plan for the closing, define desired potential action items, and have a backup plan for leaving an "open door" to meet again.

> **DEFINITIONS**
>
> **Closing frames**
> Term used to create the context, focus, or guidance that we want the listener to have for processing the content. At the end of the meeting, you will use specific closing frames.
>
> **Open door**
> A way to re-engage with the people even when the meeting is not productive or successful.

Planning the closing

Imagine the end of a meeting - a good place to start planning the closing. Optimally, a meeting would end with a positive feeling, good rapport, resolved issues and/or satisfying action items, a clear idea of next steps, and objectives that have been achieved.

This won't always happen. However, being able to imagine the meeting ending this way is a step toward achieving this goal. If you cannot even imagine it, I can promise you it won't happen. And if you *can* imagine it, you will have a much higher chance of achieving it.

Planning in advance how you are going to close the meeting can be seen as another goalpost on the path to achieving your objectives. You have already defined what you want to get out of the meeting, as well as what SOM you want everyone to be in by the end. You have defined the content of the meeting and the objections you expect, and you will make sure you have heard those objections and haven't left your customer with unanswered concerns. Now when you plan how you want to close the meeting, you leave yourself flexibility for handling the unexpected.

Planning your closing is similar to planning your content checklist:

Time: An art, not just a science

- The science refers to the general guideline that includes planning a reminder for the last 10- 15 percent of the meeting, or at least the last five minutes, for the closing. This means that for an hour-long meeting, plan to start wrapping up after 50 minutes. For a 30-minute interview, leave yourself five minutes for closing.
- The art refers to how you use your own common sense to define what is right for you in the given situation. It means using your internal radar to gauge what is happening, and having the flexibility to decide on the spot, in the most "artful" way, when to start closing the meeting.

Main points for closing

- Do not introduce any new topics during the closing. Make sure that presentations do not include new topics in the summary.
- Action Items: What are the action items I want that will help me move forward in the process? Often sales people say they will decide the actions "based on

the outcome of the meeting." But if you know what outcome you want, you can plan in advance, within reason, what action items you want to happen, and fine-tune them on the spot.

Rapport for closing

- Rapport is not constant. It changes during and between meetings, sometimes easily. One of the best ways to create rapport at the end of a meeting is to let everyone know you are at the end and starting to wrap up. This is especially important when you have a multi-person meeting and there are many presentations. If there are questions left unanswered, or objections that need to be addressed, repeat them to let your customer know you heard them. Write them down as action items and give a time by which you will answer.

Closing frames

- Frames are very important at closing to help maintain focus, especially when you are at a critical point of looking forward.

PRACTICAL USE

Using frames at closing

Closing frame: Getting ready to close

"We have about 10 minutes before we are scheduled to finish, so it's probably a good time to review our action items and see if we have anything new to add."

Backtrack frame

Review of what has been done and lead forward — "We have discussed X during the last two hours and have decided X [or wrote X action items]. Is there anything else anyone wants to mention?"

Agreement frame: Getting an agreement

"Are we all in agreement that these are the action items/next steps and time frames?"

Leaving an open door

You don't have control over the outcome of every meeting. Even after spending a lot of time planning and reviewing, things happen and you cannot always achieve your objectives.

You may find that your counterpart in the meeting is not willing to divulge any information or is showing a complete lack of interest. At an internal meeting there can be an inherent conflict that is not enabling you to move forward and is creating tensions that make you want to leave the room. At a job interview, it might be apparent that you are not right for the position, or you just do not have good chemistry with the interviewer. I'm sure if you take a moment, you will recall many meetings that did not go the way you wanted, despite your planning.

We live in a round world and you never know when you will meet or need to meet with someone again. In your personal life, you can decide not to meet people; that is your prerogative. Part of being professional is knowing that no matter what happens, you must leave an open door for doing business together, as you never know when and where you will meet again.

"Part of being professional is knowing that no matter what happens, you must leave an open door for doing business together, as you never know when and where you will meet again."

Leaving an open door is a lot about leaving your ego out of the equation. This is not easy. We are human, we have feelings, we interpret things as we do, and we have past experiences and trigger points that cause us to react in certain ways. If someone questions the integrity of what you just said, and if such an insinuation makes you furious, then in a professional situation you will have to make a choice between reacting as you normally do or maintaining a "professional" SOM, in which you react in a more appropriate manner that leaves the door open for later clarifying the real issue.

If you ever watch those audition shows on TV, you will notice the many performers who listen to the judges and just say thank you, even after they receive brutal feedback. They are trying to sell their talent, and sometimes the judges are not buying. However, those who keep their cool are leaving an open door for future opportunities.

It's more complicated in a multi-person B2B meeting. Just considering the topic of relationships, there are multiple relationships going on at every meeting — some in the room, some carried over into the room from outside experiences. There are relationships among the people in each company, and between people and their supervisors and teams. There is a relationship between the two (or more) companies, and relationships with competitors. As the leader of a meeting, it is your job to track all these relationships, and their effect on your objective, and make sure you navigate to a professional closing that leaves the door open to future business interactions among the maximum number of people.

One time, a telecom supplier introduced a new product that was cutting into the revenue of a local mobile company that was also an important customer. The local sales team decided to bring both the VP of the region and their CEO to meet the new GM of the mobile company, to show how important the mobile company was to them as a supplier and to listen to complaints and try to find a resolution.

When they got to the meeting at the mobile company, they found an enraged GM. He did not want to hear anything. He was rude and arrogant. He yelled at the local VP, calling him names in front of everyone. He ended by threatening to close down the supplier's business if they didn't cancel the product immediately.

The supplier team was in shock. Then the supplier's CEO took a moment and said to the abusive GM of the mobile company, "Let's make things clear; our company is a larger customer of your company than you are of ours. If you ever talk to any of our people the way you just did, we will move our business, which totals three times your business."

Needless to say, the mobile company GM had closed the door on a personal level to any future business with anyone in that meeting or who subsequently heard about his behavior. Even though business continued between the two companies, it was never again at the executive level. When that GM went looking for his next position, there were people he met along the way who knew of his past behavior and closed the door on him.

When you know that no matter what happens you want to leave an open door for the future, both for you personally and for your company, you will make sure to do just that.

Download the worksheet pack at http://www.dorisella.com/book
Password: 6STEPS

Worksheet 6: Closing

BUSINESS MEETINGS THAT WORK

Name of Customer _____ Date of Meeting _____

Closing

- ☐ Plan the closing
- ☐ Define desired Action Items
- ☐ Define "Leave an Open Door" strategy

How do I envision the end of the meeting? _____

At what time should I start closing the meeting? _____

Main Action Items I would like to have by end of meeting:

Topic	Date	Responsible

Closing Frames

Frame	Example	Plan
Closing Frame	We have X minutes left.	
Backtrack Frame	We have talked about X.	
Agreement Frame	Can we agree that...?	

Remember to leave an open door.

Copyright 2018 © | info@dorisella.com

GOING FORWARD

Using checklists on a daily basis

The **6-Step Checklist** is based on the premise that you should be able to prepare for every meeting quickly and naturally.

Checklists are about saving time, being more effective, and freeing important brain time to enable professionals to do what they do best. In this book, we have reviewed the six main steps of the Meeting Preparation Checklist Methodology, which is to anticipate, plan and know:

1. Your Objective
2. The Audience
3. The State of Mind (SOM)
4. Your Content
5. Potential Objections
6. How to Close the Meeting

Everything we have discussed here should be obvious to the experienced businessperson and at least make sense to the less experienced. The **6-Step Checklist** serves as a reminder, the way frequent international travelers have mental checklists so that they never leave their passport behind; otherwise they cannot get on the plane. The meeting checklist "passport" item is knowing your objectives, or you will not be able to get what you want out of a meeting.

The next most important thing after knowing your objectives is the SOM. That's like traveling without your mobile phone: You can still get on the plane, but you won't be able to function well. Being in the right SOM enables you to handle any situation, and quickly connects you to what you want to or ought to say.

The remaining items on the Checklist are also important, although the amount of time spent on them depends on such factors as the complexity of the meeting, the number of people attending, and the importance of the meeting.

In the process of writing this book, I had many conversations with sales people and heard different comments on how and when they would use this checklist. It wasn't surprising to hear from a helicopter fighter pilot who is now a CEO of a company that when things are happening quickly in the air he mentally checks the two or three critical things on his checklist and depends on himself, his pilot experience, and his wits. When he wears his CEO hat, especially when meetings are complex, he values having a full checklist to help him prepare and keep everyone focused.

An energetic medical device sales person told me, "This is all great in theory, but in everyday life I am running from meeting to meeting in the hospital. Many times I have chance meetings with doctors in the hallway." When we evaluated what consisted of a good "chance" meeting versus a poor or waste-of-time one, it was clear that it was good when she was able to bring value to the conversation and also had a follow-up plan. When we backtracked to what was in her mind before one of the good meetings she'd had, she said she knew she had wanted to create value for the doctor so that he would be more prepared to meet with her when she had something specific to sell. This was a clear objective. In these cases she has less than 30 seconds to go over her objective in her head and how she will handle the interaction, but when she knew her objective she approached others with confidence and the right SOM.

We discussed this further and realized that while she was getting ready in the morning and on her way to the hospital, she was already focused on the people she wanted to meet, and those she might meet by chance, and the key messages she wanted to share, tailored to specific people based on job functionality.

More guidelines to when and how to use checklists

This book focused on three types of examples: Comples B2B Sales meetings, Internal meetings and Job Interviews. Below are guidelines to how to use the checklists for different types of meetings.

Phone meetings and conference calls

First, to be clear — both conference calls and one-on-one phone calls are business meetings, with or without the addition of video.

Toward the end of an on-site training session I was leading, someone walked in and said that an important conference call had been moved to right now. As the topic of the call was the subject we were discussing, I was invited to stay. It was an internal business call with nine people participating, including the four sitting in the room (working on the account) and five from different HQ functions around the world.

On the call, it was not clear who was the leader or what was the objective, and the SOM of the people in the room was certainly not conducive to selling an idea internally. Only the experience of the CEO, who happened to be in the room as well, saved the customer account team from taking several steps back from their objective. Had they stopped a moment to plan and clarify their objective, even for five minutes, discussing who the people were on the call, and planning their content, they would have been much more effective.

Initial meeting complex B2B sales process

At an initial meeting, you will obviously have less information than after a process has started. Still, depending on the size of the meeting in terms of people attending and the expected length of the sales process, I recommend going over the full checklist and gathering in advance as much information on the people as you can (LinkedIn, local agents, partners, web, etc.) and on the company.

Chance meetings / coffee meetings / semi-social meetings

There is no need to go over the entire checklist for these types of meetings. At the least, though, I highly recommend defining your objective — what do you want to achieve in this interaction, and not just what do you want to say. Also, make sure you are in the right SOM to maximize the meeting. (If you have just walked out of a meeting and are feeling very annoyed, double check your personal SOM before you walk over to someone you see in the hallway.)

One-on-One meetings

If the meeting is taking place on the customer's premises, there is a good chance you will also meet other people and your customer may ask someone else to join. Even if you are going to a one-on-one meeting, it's worthwhile preparing beyond the objective and SOM, taking into consideration who else you might meet (whether you want to or not), along with whom you *want* to meet. Who is potentially critical to your objective? That includes people you don't yet know, such as a department head. It's always a good idea to have a prepared elevator pitch that is specific to your cause and that you can use at a moment's notice.

Webinar

On a webinar, not only do you need to prepare as for a regular meeting, you also have to define ways you will create attention and get feedback, as opposed to just talking into the void.

Three years ago, during a webinar training I did from Singapore for a group dispersed among different locations around Europe, I forgot to set expectations and remind them to prepare their homework the day before the meeting. Two weeks had passed since the assignment and ... guess what? Only one out of six came prepared.

For a webinar you have to prepare for all of the steps in a large meeting, and also for the technical issues. The presentation should be interactive to help keep people involved, and the speaker needs to make many pauses. Today there are programs that can show you if someone has left the webinar page and gone to a different page on their computer, which is helpful for reminding the leader to stop and engage.

Opening webcams is a great idea, but many companies don't use them and sometimes people are working from home in their sweatpants and don't want to be seen.

Will using this checklist help my bottom line?

Yes.

If you are an experienced sales person or business leader, you will use it as a reminder, especially when you are working with other people who are less experienced than you. When my daughter first learned to drive, I received a booklet from a safe driving initiative in my town letting me know where I should take her to practice making left turns, stopping at a four-way stop, navigating circles, etc. I do these things without thinking, and it would never have occurred to me that these are aspects of driving that a young driver specifically needs to continue practicing.

If you are a leader in your profession, and yet have less experience in the business world, you will notice an immediate difference in the effectiveness of your meetings.

If you have been in business for a few years, but never thought to methodically analyze what works when you have the most effective meetings, I'm sure you will be able to backtrack and find that when you were at your best, you prepared (even in your mind) according to these steps.

Any methodology is initially viewed with skepticism, especially when it is meant to be used by professional, independent, intelligent leaders.

When checklists were initially introduced to surgery, doctors perceived it as an attack on their integrity. Yet today, checklists in general are perceived by the medical community as an important tool in avoiding medical errors and decreasing complications.

We already discussed how the pilot's checklist has proved beyond doubt that it reduces mistakes and increases safety. I have every reason to believe that the **6-Step Checklist** will save time, create more efficiency, increase mindfulness by reducing worry and increase focus on core issues, ultimately increasing the bottom line.

Epilogue

It was about 20 minutes to landing in Istanbul when my plane went through the worst turbulence I have ever experienced. Normally I'm a calm passenger, but not this time. As we started our descent, I gripped the armrest and peered out the window at the whitecaps of a wild Mediterranean sea. I could see the runway and was just about to breathe a sigh of relief when I heard the familiar sound of the engines revving up, and within seconds we were sharply ascending again.

The pilot came on the speaker and explained that this was a "go-around," a procedure for when either the pilot or the tower decides it's not safe to land — usually in the case of high winds, poor visibility, or maybe an object on the runway. In this case, it was the wind.

By now, the turbulence had subsided, and just when we were all feeling comfortable, we were jolted again as the plane encountered another high-turbulence area. Then it happened again: descending toward the runway and, VROOM, swooping back up into the air. This time, all the passengers started looking at each other, checking with other people's reactions whether it was time to panic.

But this time, I wasn't disturbed. The go-around is a procedure, and for every procedure, the cockpit has a checklist. The pilots were well prepared for this type of situation. They had been through this before. Even if they hadn't, they had their checklists on hand to remind them of what to do, and in which order. The objective was clear. They knew which state of mind they needed to do their job.

I took a deep breath and sat back in my seat as we came around for the third time to a sweet, safe landing.

Acknowledgements

I am one of those people who actually likes to read acknowledgements. Ok, I don't read every name as I assume there is a lot of 'insider information', but at the same time – it always amazes me how many people are involved in making a book actually come to life.

And it begins before the first work is ever typed, with inspiration coming from different sources.

Initial inspiration

When I was a child, I was so proud that my grandfather, Harold S. Jacobson, or Bampa to everyone who knew him after I gave him that most loved name, had actually published a book that could be found in the Library of Congress. So it is befitting that my first thank you goes to my Bampa who inspired me in more ways than he could ever know.

My daughter, Maayan was a scout master-leader when she was 16. She had a team of 4 troupe leaders she supervised and every week she led a preparation meeting before the troupes met followed by a feedback meeting. As I'm sitting here writing, I'm looking at her notebook, filled with colors and stars, quotes and pasted notes. After nearly 15 years, I'm still amazed at the organization that so impressed me – " what are the objectives", " Even Feedback Sessions have an objective". I remember wishing I had her leading the long meetings I attended at work. She still inspires me every day.

My first professional boss - my father, Frank Farbenbloom, who taught me the basics of business, marketing and computers and to always be curious and look for logical connections. And as my father – is always there.

My son, Yahal, with his innate sensitivity to read people, who is always curious about those around him, encouraging and insightful help in making connections between things beyond the obvious.

Reference

Thank you to all of my friends, family and colleagues who gave insights to making the checklist and the stories more accurate and relevant; who read through drafts and gave ideas for names- Susan, Natalie, Stacy, Caron, Gadi B, Gadi M, Adar, Chen, Jacob, Noga, Anat, Daryl, Aaron, Ariel, Danny, Josh, Lisa and the many people I asked along way. My NLP teacher, Ronit Goldberg, IN & ICI President of Israel, who expected this book before I even started writing. Nancy and Sharon – Special thanks for reading and re-reading with excellent comments each time and to Dr. Benjamin Levy (Benja) for your never ending creativity and patience.

Thanks to Tsafrir, my pilot at call, for always being there to make sure I stayed accurate.

Professional

Special thanks to my cousin/author Lisa K Friedman for support and encouragement along the way, even when it wasn't so much fun to hear — but always valuable.

Michal Cooke — for taking your valuable time to give professional and personal feedback.

To my editor Jami, for being so much more than an editor.

To my fabulous designer Melinda for also giving me a boost when I needed it.

To my incredible proof reader – my one and only mother, Elaine Farbenbloom, who is always there to support me in any way needed and is still an amazing writer, editor and proof reader.

My final thanks go to my inspiring and supportive husband, Itzik who has the ability to see beyond any and every obstacle and continue to dream and achieve.

To all my family, friends and colleagues — your support and encouragement along the way has made this all happen.

References

Noam Chomsky - American linguist, philosopher, cognitive scientist, historian, social critic, and political activist.

The Challenger Sale: Taking Control of the Customer Conversation by Matthew Dixon, Brent Adamson

SPIN Selling: Situation Problem Implication Need-Payoff 1st Edition, Kindle Edition by Neil Rackham (Author)

$37 Billion

http://www.businessinsider.com/37-billion-is-lost-every-year-on-these-meeting-mistakes-2014-4

http://meetingking.com/37-billion-per-year-unnecessary-meetings-share/

Salary.com

https://business.salary.com/why-how-your-employees-are-wasting-time-at-work/slide/9/

Verizon Conferences Meetings of America

https://e-meetings.verizonbusiness.com/global/en/meetingsinamerica/meetingsinamerica_i.php

Opinion Matters Epson

https://www.newstatesman.com/business/business/2012/05/wasted-time-meetings-cost-economy-%C2%A326bn-2011

Keyorganization.com

http://www.keyorganization.com/time-management-statistics.php

Other references

https://www.inc.com/jeff-haden/why-99-percent-of-all-meetings-are-a-complete-wast.html

https://blog.lucidmeetings.com/blog/fresh-look-number-effectiveness-cost-meetings-in-us

https://www.inc.com/chris-matyszczyk/heres-how-to-calculate-how-much-money-you-waste-on-meetings.html

https://www.getminute.com/ineffective-meetings/

http://www.wolfmotivation.com/articles/the-expense-of-ineffective-meetings

About the author

During her 30+ years working around the world in both High-Tech and Service Industries, Dori Sella has developed unique ways to improve sales and marketing results by creating customized, powerful and practical tools that make an immediate impact.

Business Meetings that Work is a result of her experience facilitating and participating in thousands of meetings in over sixty countries with hundreds of different companies, both global conglomerates and start-ups.

In addition to holding positions as VP Marketing and Sales Consultant, Dori has formal education in Marketing, Social Work, NLP Trainer, Coaching, SPIN, TAS, and TOC. She speaks several languages and has spoken at numerous professional conferences around the world.

Dori is always looking for practical ways to be more efficient while balancing a diverse and full lifestyle that includes many interests – foremost her family. She is an avid folk-dancer and understands the importance of knowing the steps and the flow of the dance. She loves helping businesses find the steps they need to flow towards their goals.

Stay in touch

www.Dorisella.com

https://www.facebook.com/Dorisella.author/

www.linkedin.com/in/dorisella

INDEX

A

action items, 11, 22, 36, 57, 87, 121-125

alignment, 11, 43, 56-60

attendees, 3, 11, 26-27, 30, 44, 61, 67-68, 74, 109

B

body language, 33, 60, 73-76, 79

business meeting, 4-5, 7, 17, 107

C

checklist, 1-5, 7-11, 25, 57, 71, 80, 119, 123, 131-132, 134-135, 137-138, 140, 142

closing, 11, 20, 52, 75, 121-125, 127

Complex B2B, 8, 10, 19-21, 29, 35, 40, 44-45, 47-48, 53-54, 57, 62, 86, 89-90, 134

content, 11, 19, 25, 30, 32, 60, 68-69, 79-80, 82-84, 86-88, 93-94, 101-102, 113, 122-123, 131, 134

customer, 2, 7, 10-11, 17-21, 25, 29, 32-34, 38, 40, 43-51, 53-54, 58-59, 61, 66, 68, 70, 73, 84-86, 94, 98, 109, 114-116, 122, 124, 127-128, 134-135, 145

E

expectations, 11, 27, 38, 43, 61-62, 82, 94-95, 103, 136

F

flexibility, 19, 27, 67-68, 83, 94, 115, 117, 123

Frames, 11, 80, 102-104, 122, 124-125

G

Google, 32, 100

I

internal alignment, 11, 43, 56-57

Internal attendees, 44

Internal meeting, 8, 10, 22, 30, 36, 40, 44, 50, 54-55, 59, 62, 84, 87, 90, 126

J

Job interview, 8, 10, 23, 31, 37, 41, 44, 51, 55, 60, 62, 84, 88, 91, 104, 109, 116, 126

language patterns, 11, 107-108, 113, 119

L

leader, 17, 26-27, 50, 53, 56-58, 70, 72, 107, 115, 127, 134, 136-137

LinkedIn, 27, 32, 51, 134, 148

M

metaphors, 96, 100

N

non-verbal cues, 93

O

objections, 11, 33, 35, 52, 67, 69, 76, 92, 98, 103, 107-115, 117, 119, 122, 124, 131

objectives, 3, 11, 15, 17-19, 21-24, 26-32, 35, 37-38, 44-46, 49, 56-58, 62, 66, 79-80, 83-84, 90, 95-96, 122, 126, 132, 142

open door, 11, 121-122, 126-128

P

pilots, 1, 3, 140

Plan B, 11, 15-16, 38-40

professional meeting, 7

Q

questions, 2, 11, 31, 33, 37-39, 45-46, 49, 52, 58, 60, 73, 76, 82-84, 86, 89-92, 95, 104, 107, 112, 114, 116-117, 124, 127

R

rapport, 11, 30, 69, 80, 83, 92-97, 102, 111, 116-117, 122, 124

relationship, 6-7, 17-18, 25, 44-47, 61, 81, 127

S

sales, 2, 4-10, 16, 18-21, 24, 27, 29, 32, 35, 38, 40-41, 44, 47-49, 53-54, 56-57, 62, 67-68, 71, 75, 81-82, 84-86, 90, 92-94, 98, 101, 104, 107, 109, 111, 123, 127, 132-134, 137, 147 small talk, 33, 75, 81, 92-93

SOM, 11, 65-76, 79, 84, 92, 94, 96-98, 102-103, 107, 109, 117, 122, 127, 131-135

stories, 11, 17, 54, 81, 88, 92, 96, 98, 100-101, 107, 142

success criteria, vii, 11, 15, 32-33, 35-37

T

time, 2-6, 9, 11, 18-20, 25, 38, 40-41, 45, 56-59, 65, 67-68, 72, 76, 79-84, 92, 95-97, 99, 101, 103, 108-110, 114-117, 119, 121, 123-127, 131-132, 138-143

Made in the USA
San Bernardino, CA
16 June 2019